FROM THE CREATION TO REVELATION

By the same author:

Poetry

A Rhyming History of Britain: 55BC–AD1966
Shakespeare in a Nutshell: A Rhyming Guide to All the Plays
*The Cosmic Verses: A Rhyming History of the Universe**

Astronomy

The Sun's Family
Astronomy with Binoculars
The Amateur Astronomer's Handbook
Astronomy for Amateurs
Guide to Astronomy
Beginner's Guide to Astronomical Telescope Making
Young Astronomer's Handbook
Astronomy Handbook
Pocket Book of Astronomy
How to Use an Astronomical Telescope
Astronomy with a Small Telescope
Stars and Planets
How Do We Know Einstein Is Right?

Fiction

Space Intruder
The Moon-Winners

*PUBLISHED BY MICHAEL O'MARA BOOKS LIMITED

JAMES MUIRDEN

FROM THE CREATION TO REVELATION

Illuminations by
DAVID ECCLES

Michael O'Mara Books Limited

A CIP catalogue record for this book is available from the British Library

Papers used by Michael O'Mara Books Limited are natural, recyclable products made from wood grown in sustainable forests. The manufacturing processes conform to the environmental regulations of the country of origin.

ISBN: 978-1-84317-259-8

1 3 5 7 9 10 8 6 4 2

Designed and typeset by www.glensaville.com

Printed and bound in Finland by WS Bookwell

Contents

For the many people
who mean to read the Bible sometime,
hoping that it will encourage them to do so
before it is too late.

INTRODUCTION

Some years ago, I wrote *A Rhyming History of Britain* in order to teach myself some history. I embarked on *The Rhyming Bible* in order to teach myself something about the Bible, which is, after all, the most influential book of the Western world.

As far as I can find out, there has been no attempt at a rhyming overview (as opposed to versified 'highlights') since the *Central Franconian Rhyming Bible*, an early twelfth-century work that has survived only as a fragment. Things might have been different if the Hebrews had used rhyme as an aid to memory. The bulk of the Old Testament was probably written at about the same time as Homer wrote (or dictated) *The Iliad* and *The Odyssey*, and it has been natural for his translators to render them into verse form. If the Old Testament had originated as a rhyming epic, it would still be admired as 'literature' today. Instead, the Bible must hold the record as the least-read book of modern times in relation to its impressive sales.

Compression means selection, but I have tried to avoid ending up with a series of 'highlights' unrelated by cause and effect. This is much easier to do in the case of the Old Testament, where genealogy drives the narrative. Genesis and Exodus chronicle the time from the Creation to the arrival of the Israelites at the borders of the Promised Land – Canaan. Leviticus, Numbers and Deuteronomy are concerned mainly with admin and family records, and do not advance the story by more than a few years, but with Joshua the narrative continues (one might say) with a vengeance. Judges, Ruth, Samuel, Kings and Chronicles (Chronicles duplicates much of Kings, sometimes word for word), take the story to the fall of Jerusalem in 586 BC. After these, the continuity is broken: we have the Books of the Exile and Return, some historical (such as Ezra and Nehemiah) and some prophetic, such as Isaiah.

A sequential overview of the New Testament is not so easy. Its scribes were trying to collate a mass of (probably) secondhand or thirdhand information about Jesus's brief ministry and its confused aftermath, all of which was coloured by his reported assurance that the Second Coming – the Day of Judgment – would occur during their own lifetime. None of them could have dreamed that what they wrote would be held sacred two thousand years later, since they were convinced that the world of themselves and their forefathers would soon be no more! The Gospels strike me as a form of apocalyptic journalism, while the Epistles (or letters) anticipate our own 'End is Nigh' pamphleteers.

We do not know who the scribes were, but it is likely that they were writing these texts for different communities, embryonic churches of Christ located around the eastern Mediterranean. It is possible or even probable that the energetic Paul had been involved in these churches' early development, if not in their foundation. And it is with respect to Paul that the arrangement of Books in the New Testament misleads. Some of his Epistles, such as the First Letter to the Thessalonians, are almost certainly the earliest 'Christian' writings, predating any of the Gospels. There is a case for supposing that the image of Jesus as 'a light to lighten the Gentiles' is based on Paul's interpretation rather than on the Lord's teaching, since the Gospel-writers, who may not have put pen to papyrus until three or more decades after Jesus's death, must by that time have been heavily influenced by Paul's views. If this is the case, they had to square a most awkward circle. How could they reconcile Jesus's reported statements that Gentiles were dogs (Mark 7:27), and that the disciples should preach their message only to the Jews (Matthew 10:5), with the Pauline doctrine that Christ died for all mankind?

Some Gospel accounts of the same event differ so much that a 'collated' account is impossible. In the more important instances I have presented the different versions for comparison. Readers may not, for example, be aware that according to Matthew's Gospel Jesus was born at his parents' home, since they lived in Bethlehem! The four versions of the Resurrection appearances also differ greatly – the only fact that they appear to agree on is that Mary Magdalene (alone or accompanied) was the first to see the risen Lord.

I am only too well aware of how much has had to be left out; but if my efforts make you think that the Bible might in fact be a good read rather than just a source of good readings, I ask no more. All human life is there; of the heavenly life, it is for others to speak.

Two books have proved most helpful during these enjoyable labours: *Jesus,* by A. N. Wilson (Pimlico, 2003), and *Reading the Bible,* by John Weightman (Weech Publishing, 2003).

JAMES MUIRDEN

PART 1

THE OLD TESTAMENT

PROLOGUE

THE CREATION: Genesis 1–2

Day 1

To make the world, God worked a six-day week –
an effort of unsparing dedication!
These are the first words that we hear Him speak:
'Let's throw some light upon the situation.'

Day 2

So Day and Night began. Then He decided,
since everything was formless H_2O,
to have the waters tidily divided –
the sky above, the boundless deep below.

Day 3

This was a busy day! He first explained
that all the waters underneath the sky
should come together. Once the rest had drained,
he waited briefly for the land to dry...

...and said: 'With all this space, I'll introduce
a novel range of vegetable matter –
trees, plants, etcetera. They will reproduce
and flourish, through the seeds they set and scatter.'

Day 4

He made the sun, to measure out each day;
the moon and stars, to count the months and years.
(I must admit, I'm puzzled at the way
He made the day before the sun appears!)

Day 5

He stocked the empty oceans and the air
with every fish and bird He could invent.
'I want to see you spreading everywhere.
So go ahead – it's your environment!'

Day 6

To populate the landmass, He created
the many creatures that we see today:
the useful ones, to be domesticated;
the lower orders, and the Beasts of Prey...

...and then, to rule the land and sky and sea
now teeming with the life He had prepared,
our Maker introduced Humanity
(both genders in His image), and declared:

'I give you lordship over all Creation...
the seeds and fruits of harvest you will eat.
The others will make do with Vegetation.
I think that's all – my Project is complete!'

Day 7

Six days He'd laboured very hard indeed,
so on this day He took a well-earned rest.
This is the reason why the Lord decreed
that every week the Seventh Day is blessed.

CHAPTER 1

FROM ADAM TO ABRAHAM (Genesis 2–22)

ADAM AND EVE: Genesis 2*

* This is an alternative version of the Creation of mankind to that in Gen 1; in the Prologue, men and women were created simultaneously on Day 6.

The Lord chose Eden as His base –
at that time an unspoilt place.
He planted groves of fruitful trees,
and in the evenings took His ease
strolling beneath their pleasant shade.
It needed tending, so He made
the first man, Adam, out of dust,
breathed life into him, and discussed

the terms on which he was employed.
'Eat what you fancy, but avoid
the Tree of Knowledge over there –
its fruit is fatal, so take care!'
To keep its acres trimmed and weeded
an under-gardener was needed,
and so the Lord gave him a mate,
who'd also help him propagate.
Taking a rib while Adam dozed

(the wound miraculously closed),
Eve was created, bare as he;
but this full-frontal nudity
caused no embarrassment at all.
Such innocence, before the Fall!

THE FALL OF MAN: Genesis 3

A Serpent, sent there to deceive,
began to use its arts on Eve,
who fell for its persuasive patter.
It hissed: 'That warning doesn't matter
about the fruit that's on the Tree –
it's Educational, you see.
What's wrong with wanting to be wise?
Behold the world with open eyes!'
Her husband also had a bite –
it opened up their eyes all right...
'It's shocking – you've got nothing on!'
'Neither have you!' Their blindness gone,
some fig leaves helped to hide their shame;
but then the Lord called Adam's name.
'Why are you hiding? Does this mean
you've eaten from the Tree? Come clean!'

Adam blamed Eve; Eve blamed the snake;
and God in threefold judgment spake.
'Serpent, be Man's accursed foe –
forever lowest of the low!'
To Eve: 'I was a devotee
of sexual equality –
but this has made me think again.
Henceforth, you will be ruled by men!'
To Adam: 'You will dig and hoe
a stony, unproductive row,
hoping to meet your daily needs
despite the thistles and the weeds...
and when you die, as die you must,
your body will revert to dust!'
So through the Garden gate they went,
from Eden's groves to banishment...

CAIN AND ABEL: Genesis 4

Their first son, Cain, was made to till the ground;
the second, Abel, kept the livestock tended.
The time to make their Offerings came round...
when He saw Cain's, the Lord was much offended.

'You haven't tried!' He said. 'Abel comes first!'
So Cain killed Abel in a fit of passion.
God said: 'Depart! Henceforth you are accursed –
I can't have people acting in this fashion!'

Cain groaned: 'How will I manage on my own?
People will hunt me down, and murder me!'
'I'll brand you – then they'll leave you well alone!'
So Cain survived, and raised a family.

NOAH AND THE FLOOD: Genesis 6–8

Eight generations after the Creation,
God viewed his handiwork with consternation.
'Mankind's corrupt, and sinking ever lower...
the only person I can trust is Noah.

I'll start again, with him!' So He decided
to send a Flood. Noah had been provided
with all he needed to construct a boat
or Ark, to keep his family afloat,
which also had sufficient space to spare

to let him take a procreative pair
of every kind of insect, bird or beast
(the fish did not mind water in the least).
For forty days and nights it simply poured:
all forms of life were drowned, save those aboard
the drifting Ark, in which were packed away
the only samples of their DNA!

The waters fell, the vessel came to rest,
and Noah sent a dove out, as a test –
the olive leaf it brought back in its beak
showed that, elsewhere, the Flood had passed its peak.
Some patient waiting till the ground was dry...
and Man emerged, to have another try!

GOD'S COVENANT WITH ABRAHAM: Genesis 15

The race of *Semites* was begun
by Shem. As Noah's second son
he started off a male line
whose generation No. 9

(three hundred years after the Ark),
resulted in the Patriarch*
called Abraham. He had a vision

* A 'father figure', like Jacob and Moses.

in which God mentioned His decision
to make his heirs the Chosen Race.
'Today you move from place to place,'
God told him, 'but these wandering ways
will lead to a more settled phase
when your heirs put down roots instead –
in Canaan (bordering the Med),
although that won't occur just yet –
four hundred years of toil and sweat
await you, in a foreign land.'
'That's fine; but I don't understand
how this can be – we've not been blessed
with children, though we've done our best!'
'A nation I have promised you –
and all my promises come true!'
To seal the bargain they had made,
he felt the circumcision blade
remove his foreskin,* as, by law,
all males would for evermore,
to signify that they agreed
to serve the Lord in word and deed.

* 17:10.

SARAH LAUGHS: Genesis 16–17

Sarah, his wife, had started to despair –
at her age there was no way she'd conceive.
'My servant Hagar's young, and she might bear...
So try your luck with her – I give you leave!'

Still young at eighty-six, the plan worked fine,
and Ishmael was born. Thirteen years passed;
then God said: 'Even though you're ninety-nine,
Sarah will bless you with a son at last!'

Though Abraham expressed some reservation,
and aged Sarah laughed at such a plan,
she did indeed bear Isaac (in translation
this means *He's laughing*). Problems now began...

...and Sarah banished Hagar and her child.
The Lord sought anxious Abraham, and said:
'I'll see they're well looked after in the wild –
Isaac's the one from whom your race will spread...

...but your first-born will also found a nation.'
And Ishmael did – he had twelve sons in all.
The Muslims treat his name with veneration,
for, through his line, the Prophet heard the Call.

TROUBLE WITH LOT: Genesis 18–19

While Abraham enjoyed the country air,
and wandered with his herdsmen here and there,
his nephew Lot, no camper, much preferred
the Cities of the Plain (you will have heard
of Sodom and Gomorrah's reputation!).

The Lord was bent on their incineration,
but Abraham was bold in their defence:
'Lord, kindly save the righteous residents!'
God thought the matter over, and agreed:
'If there are fifty, then I won't proceed!'
'Say there are forty-five – what happens then?'
Eventually they compromised on ten,
but since no righteous people could be found,
plans went ahead to burn them to the ground.
Two Angels called on Lot, who was his kin,
and told him of the plight that he was in...
'Clear off with those to whom you are related –
don't look back, or you'll be annihilated!'
The Lord rained brimstone on these pits of hell,
which naturally burned extremely well;
but Lot's wife simply *had* to see the sight,
which turned her into salt – and serve her right.

ISAAC SURVIVES THE KNIFE: Genesis 22

The Lord called Abraham, to say:
'I want some sacrificial act.

I've got your son in mind, in fact.
So get the necessaries packed –
you're leaving right away.'

Hard to imagine his distress!
But even so, he didn't cry,
or seek to know the reason why
his dearest Isaac had to die –
he simply answered 'Yes'.

He couldn't share this crushing blow –
just took the things he would require
to slay his son and light the fire:
the two of them climbed ever higher
above the plain below.

Then Isaac said: 'I cannot see
the lamb that you're supposed to slay.'
His frantic father had to say:
'It isn't very far away –
God's kept this lamb for me!'

He built an altar; on it laid
the sticks to burn, then seized his heir,
and bound him fast, and set him there
upon the wood. His neck was bare
and ready for the blade...

An Angel hurtled down, and said:
'Don't cut his throat! You've passed the test!
You've proved to God you love Him best;
through you, all nations will be blessed!'
He slew a ram instead.

CHAPTER 2

JACOB AND HIS TWELVE SONS (Genesis 23–50)

THE GO-BETWEEN: Genesis 24

The Canaan folk, where Abraham pitched camp,
seem friendly; so he tells his right-hand man:
'I'm worried stiff in case some local vamp
should grab my son – that's *not* part of my plan!

'I'm getting old, so grasp my thigh and swear
that you will choose the lad a Hebrew bride...
Cross the Euphrates, find my kinsfolk there,
and bring one back – I leave you to decide!'

The steward answers: 'Just one question, sir...
She may refuse to leave her native land.
Should I return and take your son to her?'
His master thunders: 'Don't you understand?

'The Lord, the God of Heaven, swore to me
(as Procreator of the Chosen Race)
that we'd receive, in perpetuity,
mellifluous Canaan as our Promised Place!

'If she's intent on staying where she is,
the oath you swear will then be null and void.
I've claimed this land – I mean it to be his,
so if he leaves, I shall be most annoyed!'

The faithful steward sets out on his trip,
reaches the place, and sits down by a well.

'The one whom I importune for a sip
will serve my camels too – that's how I'll tell!'

Enter Rebecca, shouldering her pot...
'Sir, have a drink! Your beasts seem thirsty too!'
She fills the trough: the camels drink the lot.
The steward asks her straight out: 'Who are you?'

'The daughter of Bethuel, Nahor's* son.
Your beasts (and you) are welcome for the night.'
The steward bows, and thinks: 'She is the one!
Lord, you have heard my master's prayer all right!'

* Abraham's brother.

He slips a golden bracelet on each wrist;
a golden ring he clips on to her nose.
(Rebecca, we assume, does not resist!)
The moment she's been gilded, off she goes...

...to tell her folk, and flaunt her decoration.
The steward and her brother Laban meet.
A flurry of intense negotiation,
and that same night the bargain is complete!

GRIPPING STUFF: Genesis 25:21–26

Their marriage had been consummated,
so Isaac and Rebecca waited
to see what they had propagated...
But nothing ever came!

Now twenty unblest years had passed.
'God, help her!' Isaac prayed at last.
'The two of us are ageing fast –
and she will take the blame!'

God did what only God can do...
Rebecca's waistline grew and grew,
and soon she felt not one but *two*.
'Thanks, Lord, but all the same...

'...my babies fight incessantly!
This jostling's not good for me!'
The Lord replied: 'Your progeny
are arguing their claim.

'You've got two nations growing there.
The second child that you bear
will take his older brother's share.'
When their joint birthday came...

...Esau was first to see the light.
A hairy thing, his heel gripped tight
by brother Jacob. What a sight!
Henceforth, Rebecca's aim...

...was to promote her second son,
who would, God said, be No. 1.
She didn't care how this was done –
she'd play a ruthless game!

Then one day hungry Esau said:
'That stew's so tempting, rich and red!
I want some, Jacob, plus some bread –
I'm starving!' 'Just proclaim...

... to all the world your birthright's mine,
and you can eat.' 'It smells divine,'
said Esau. 'Yes, of course I'll sign
and put it in your name!'

SMOOTH OPERATOR: Genesis 27:1–41

Isaac had aged, and grew opaque of eye.
He said to Esau: 'Go and hunt some dinner.
I'll eat it, then I'll bless you, then I'll die.'
Rebecca heard... ambition burned within her.

She said to Jacob: 'Quick! We'll do a switch!
I'll cook a tasty dish, which you'll provide
in Esau's name. He won't know which is which!'
'He will,' said Jacob. 'Esau's hairy hide...

'...is nothing like this velvet skin of mine,
for I'm a smooth man.' 'This is what we'll do,'
his mother said, 'I'll get some lengths of twine
and fasten bits of goatskin on to you!'

She dressed the lad in Esau's pungent gear,
and Isaac sniffed. 'How sweet you smell to me!
And yet – you sound like Jacob, to my ear.'
'You're crazy, Dad. Enjoy your fricassee!'

So Isaac blessed him as his firstborn son.
'God send you all the food and drink you need!
Your nation will be feared by everyone,
and those who curse you will be cursed indeed!'

Then Esau turned up. 'Father, bless your heir!'
'I've blessed you once already!' Isaac said.
The penny dropped... 'You blessed *him*! That's unfair!
He's pinched what's due to me – bless me instead!'

'Alas, my son,' Isaac replied, distressed,
'it makes no difference how it came about.
You'll serve your brother Jacob, now he's blessed.'
But Esau swore an oath to sort him out...

BEGETTING: Genesis 27:42–30:24

1. Family planning

Rebecca said to Jacob: 'Go!
Esau is dangerous, you know!
My brother Laban's place will do
until he makes it up with you.'
She talked to Isaac, who agreed.
'Marry a cousin, start to breed
and multiply, and raise a nation!
God made a solemn proclamation
to Abraham your grandpapa
(and led him and his flocks this far),
declaring that this fertile place
is destined for His chosen race.
One day it will be in our hands –
till then, reside in other lands!'

2. Jacob's Ladder

He set off. When the sun had set
(he hadn't crossed the Jordan yet)
he chose, out of a vast selection,
a stone of suitable cross-section
to form a pillow for his head,
and dreamed his Dream. A Ladder led
from earth to Heaven without bending,
Angels ascending and descending
as though it was an escalator.
He saw, beyond it, the Creator...
'In case you don't know who I am,
behold the God of Abraham
and Isaac! This land where you rest,
the regions to the east and west
and north and south I give to you;
but you must take a long-term view.

Marry, and start a dynasty
that burgeons exponentially!'
Jacob believed this augured well,
and called his resting-place *Bethel*.*

* 'The House of God'.

3. The switch

He reached his Uncle Laban's place,
saw cousin Rachel's lovely face,
and *Zap*! – he was infatuated.
The terms his uncle stipulated
were these: he'd make the ardent boy
work seven years in his employ,
and then would come the wedding night...
Her veil hid her face from sight
when joyful Jacob took his bride –
but when he woke, there at his side
was Leah, Rachel's elder sister!

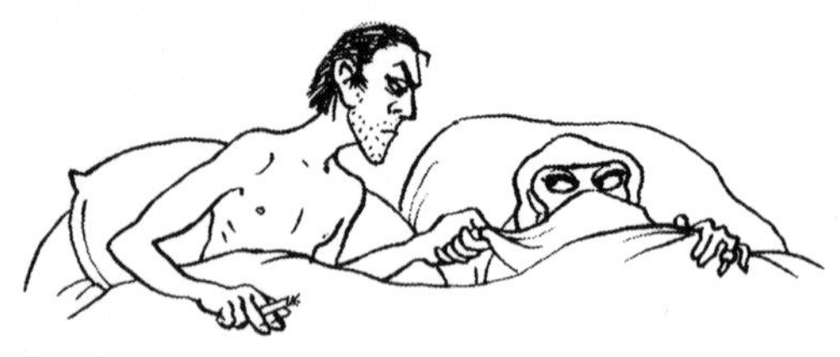

He told his uncle: 'You're a twister!
I didn't mean to marry *her*!'
'I daresay not, but we prefer
to wed our girls sequentially.
You've married Leah, so Rachel's free.
Next week she can be yours on credit;
as for your payment, shall we spread it
across another seven-year plan?'
He was a doubly-married man...

4. Jacob's progeny

It would be hard to document
the goings-on in Jacob's tent –
the tension must have been terrific!
Leah, exceedingly prolific,
had six sons, and a daughter, Dinah;
so Rachel started to malign her,
and turned upon her husband too:
'I'm childless all because of you!'
Jacob replied: 'I've done my best –
it's up to God to do the rest!'
'All right, then – here's my handmaid Bilhah.
You've my permission to fulfil her,
if you will say her sons are mine!'
This surrogate device worked fine,
so Leah, rather jealous, said

Leah bore Reuben, Simeon, Levi, Judah, Issachar and Zebulun, plus Dinah.

Bilhah bore Dan and Naphtali.

that he could take *her* maid* to bed,
and Gad and Asher were produced.
At last poor Rachel's womb was loosed...
Joseph, the first son she begot,
would prove the greatest of the lot!

* Zilpah.

UNNATURAL SELECTION: Genesis 30:25–31:21

'Uncle Laban,' said Jacob, 'time's urgently pressing.
I've worked out my contract, you know,
and I want to be off!' 'But you've brought me God's blessing.
I'll put up your wages – don't go!'

But Jacob was cunning... 'I know what we'll do.
You can pay me in goats and in sheep.
You will own all the best (of a uniform hue),
and the ones that are speckled, I'll keep!'

This was done. All the livestock, white, speckled and dark,
were divided and carefully checked.
From some branches of trees he removed strips of bark,
which gave them a speckled effect...

...that the animals saw at the moment of mating.
Thus, Laban's immaculate ewes,
despite their perfection, could not help creating
striped offspring, for Jacob to choose!

And he added selective controls of his own...
His branches he showed to the best,
but the ones that were feeble, he left well alone.
So as you have probably guessed...

...his speckled flocks thrived, but his uncle's did not;
and Laban's sons didn't approve.
'He's ruined our father, and taken the lot!'
So Jacob decided to move...

JACOB WRESTLES WITH GOD: Genesis 31:22–33:20

It turned into a ten-day race...
His outraged in-laws soon gave chase
and overtook him at a place
near Jericho!*

* Mizpah.

But God spoke a restraining word
which Uncle Laban must have heard,
for nothing violent occurred.
Jacob could go...

But now he was extremely scared!
What trap might Esau have prepared?
Could things between them be repaired?
His stock was low!

He sent his choicest beasts ahead.
'If Esau comes, they're his!' he said.
Crossing the Jabbok River's bed,*
a nameless foe...

* Tributary of the Jordan.

...attacked him just before the ford
(he'd stayed back of his own accord).
He never guessed it was the Lord –
how could he know?

To lessen Jacob's fearful grip,
God touched the socket on his hip,
so that his joint began to slip.
But even so...

...the wrestling went on all night,
and pain-racked Jacob held on tight.

The Lord said: 'Now it's getting light,
please let me go!'

'Then bless me, friend!' 'You fought so well,
you shall be known as *Israel*.'*
From which the weary man could tell
who'd been his foe!

* 'He wrestles with God.'

Esau received him. 'I can see
you've raised yourself a family!
Why offer all these flocks to me?
Please keep them!' 'No...

'...a little present, brother dear!'
So back went Esau to Seir,*
but Israel thought: 'I'll settle here.†
You never know...'

* Esau's town in Edom.

† Various places are mentioned (e.g. Succoth, Bethel and Shechem), before Israel ended up at Hebron, where Isaac lived.

BLOOD BROTHER: Genesis 37

Our story now moves on a bit...
Joseph, his father's favourite
(since he was Rachel's first-born son*)
considered himself No. 1,
and sported quite a flashy cloak,
which marked him out from lesser folk.
He told his brothers: 'All of you
bowed down to me (our father too)
in my prognosticating dream!'
His jealous siblings hatched a scheme
to kill him, dump him out of sight,
and blame their darling brother's plight
on some carnivorous intruder.
But Reuben and his brother Judah

* She died giving birth to her second son, Benjamin (35:16–20).

objected: 'It is wrong to slay
our flesh and blood, our DNA!'
They therefore kept his cloak, and sold
the chilly seventeen-year-old
to traders needing things to sell
in Egypt, and who paid quite well.*
This done, they went and slit the throat
of some unprofitable goat,
bloodied the cloak, and took it back
as proof of sanguinous attack.
'A wild beast has savaged him,
and torn my poor boy limb from limb!'
wailed Israel. 'No, do not try
to comfort me – just let me die!'
Joseph was sold in the bazaar
to Pharaoh's captain, Potiphar...

* Twenty shekels of silver.

A WOMAN SCORNED: Genesis 39

A first-class slave, he slaved away,
enjoying increased rank (and pay)
until he made a fatal slip
that finished off his stewardship.
When Mrs Potiphar proposed
some business while her husband dozed,
her forwardness was not returned.
The lady, shocked at being spurned,
pulled off his cloak, found Mr P.,
and cried: 'He tried to ravish me,
and ran off, leaving this behind!'

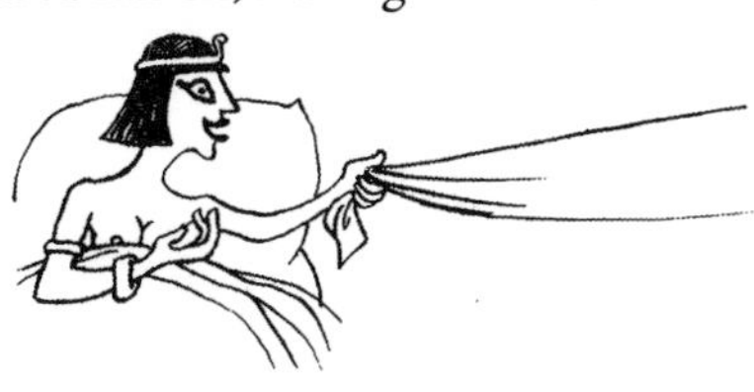

His reputation undermined,
Joseph was locked up by his master.
But God wrought Triumph from Disaster...

THE FAT AND THE LEAN: Genesis 40:1–41:40

Two years passed under lock and key.
Then Pharaoh dreamed disturbingly,
and experts from all quarters met
to solve this violent vignette...
'Out of the Nile came seven cows,
sleek, well-fed, which began to browse
upon the reeds. And then – guess what?
A most emaciated lot
(seven again) came out as well,
and ate them up. Come on – foretell!'
They couldn't (as you would expect!);
then one* said: 'Sire, with respect,
a fellow whom I knew in jail
could read such omens without fail –
he foresaw that you'd let me out,
because of what I'd dreamed about!'
Joseph was tidied up, and brought
before the Pharaoh and his court.
'God's given you a vital clue
to what He is about to do,
if this dream is correctly read,'
the thirty-year-old Hebrew said.
'The seven fat cows signify
as many years when yields are high;
then you will have a seven-year spell
when famine grips the country.' 'Well,'
said Pharaoh, 'since you've seen so far,
what now?' 'Appoint a Famine Tsar

* Pharaoh's cup-bearer.

(responsible to you alone)
who'll take a fifth of all that's grown
and store it up to keep things going
during the years when nothing's growing.'
Pharaoh replied: 'It's pretty clear
that you alone, of all those here,
are competent to see things through.
So as of now, it's up to you
to make sure that the system works –
you'll get a wife and car,* plus perks.'

* An archaic word for a chariot.

PLAYING GAMES: Genesis 42:1–43:14

The famine hit the Middle East,
and hardship rapidly increased,
so people started making tracks
to Egypt, taking empty sacks.
Joseph was gob-smacked to behold
those brothers who had had him sold
among the hungry people queuing.

He acted tough... 'What are you doing?
You're spies!' 'Oh, mighty lord, we're not!'
'There's ten of you – is that the lot?'
'No, lord – one brother is deceased.
The other one (the last and least),

called Benjamin, remained behind
with Father.' 'One of you I'll bind,'
he said, selecting Simeon;
'as for the rest of you, be gone,
and bring your younger brother here
when you come back for more next year!'
They went off with supplies of grain,
agreeing to return again
with Benjamin; but Israel said:
'Now Simeon's as good as dead
(like dearest Joseph) I will *not*
send Benjamin – he's all I've got
that my beloved Rachel bore!'
Their grain ran out; they needed more
to see them through the coming season,
and Israel at last saw reason.
'Oh, take my last son if you must,
and pray that this great lord is just!'

RELOCATION, RELOCATION, RELOCATION: Genesis 43:15–50:26

This time, after some further fun,
Joseph came clean. 'I am the one
you sold into captivity!
Don't be embarrassed – I can see
that God in fact encouraged you,
for five more cornless years are due,
and I have got sufficient clout
to bring you and your households out.
So set about it straight away –
and plan for an extended stay!'
The Lord told Israel in a vision
that this would be the right decision:

'Go down to Egypt, settle there.
Don't worry, you'll be in my care!
Once you have grown into a nation,
I'll organise your re-migration.'
So Israel's entire clan
formed one extensive caravan,
and left the Promised Land behind.
The Pharaoh was extremely kind,
and found them a well-watered place
in Goshen, which became their base.
So seventeen swift years went by...
Then Israel, about to die,
called all his sons to him, and said:
'Please take me back, when I am dead,
to Canaan (sorry it's so far)
and bury me at Machpelah,*
where Abraham, and Isaac too,
are laid – that would be kind of you!'
Embalming him before the rites.
took forty days and forty nights –
no question here of cutting corners.
There were innumerable mourners,
and Pharaoh's household went as well
to bury fruitful Israel.
So Joseph, in effect, became
his brothers' lord in all but name,
though Chapter 50 does imply
he was among the first to die.
'In sands of Egypt bury me –
but dig me up eventually,
and take me back with you, to rest
in Canaan's earth, which God has blessed.'

* Location unknown.

Israel died aged 147.

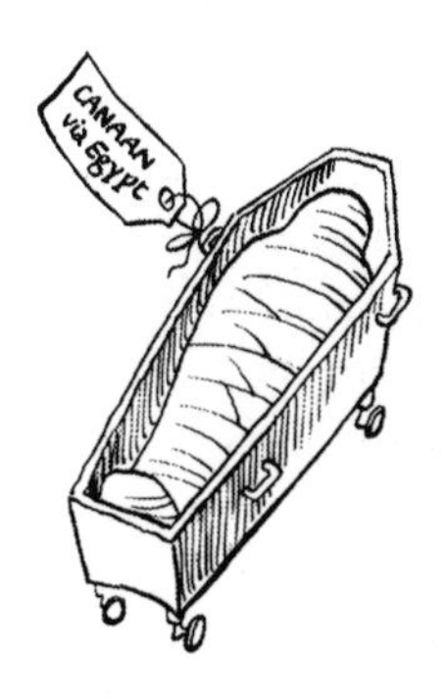

A NOTE ON THE TWELVE TRIBES OF ISRAEL

Jacob (Israel) had twelve sons by his two wives and two concubines, but only ten of these founded territorial tribes in their name. The exceptions were Levi and Joseph.

The descendants of Levi became the priestly sect (Levites), who were not given territory in Canaan, but owned certain pasturelands.

Joseph had two sons by his wife Asenath, the daughter of the Priest of Heliopolis. These were Manasseh and Ephraim. Israel demanded that these two grandsons be considered as part of his own sons' generation. This brings the total back to twelve.

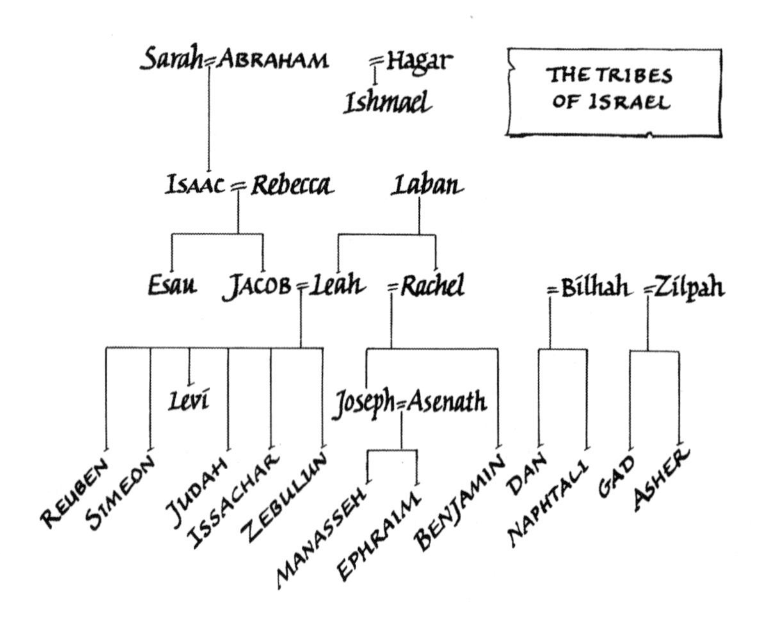

CHAPTER 3

MOSES AND THE EXODUS (Exodus – Deuteronomy)

GENDER SELECTION: Exodus 1:1–2:10

The honeymoon was all too brief, of course...
They were downgraded to a labour force
producing bricks from mud (or they could opt

for working in the fields till they dropped).
But still their numbers rose, and Pharaoh feared
they'd change sides if an enemy appeared.
To keep their growing numbers within bounds,
he told the midwives:* 'When you're on your rounds,
kill every male as it leaves the womb!'
But this did not affect the Baby Boom,
since neither midwife followed his instruction.
'I haven't noticed any great reduction,'
said Pharaoh. 'Has my edict been ignored?
Why have you let them live?' 'It's like this, lord –
these Hebrew wives give birth at such a rate,

* Shiphrah and Puah.

however quick we are, we're always late!'
'Well, once a child is born, if it's a male,
please throw it in the Nile, without fail!'

BULLRUSH BABY: Exodus 2:1–10

A Levite's wife called Jochebed
bore Moses, and you will have read
about the risks she had to run
to save their threatened three-month son.
A buoyant basket met her needs,
and Moses floated in the reeds,
while not far off, his sister hid,
saw Pharaoh's daughter lift the lid,

and boldly said: 'I think I know
a Hebrew nurse who'd suit him.' 'Go
and find her!' ordered the princess.
The scam was a complete success.
'I'll pay you well,' the princess said
to Moses' mother Jochebed;
and when the little lad had grown,
the royals raised him as their own...

BURNING BUSH, TANGLED TONGUE: Exodus 2:11–4:17

This tongue-tied youth's defining act
was when he lost his cool, and whacked
an overseer, which, in fact,
knocked the oppressor dead!

To stop the body being found
he buried it in sandy ground,
but soon the word had got around –
a price was on his head!

In Midian* he thought he'd dwell.
He helped some maidens by a well...
In less time than it takes to tell,
to one of them he's wed!

* Western Arabia.

Zipporah, daughter of Jethro.

One day a strange event occurred.
His father-in-law owned a herd
which Moses tended. 'How absurd!
That bush is burning red...

...but it is not consumed!' God spoke
within the bush, amidst the smoke:
'You will throw off your people's yoke
and lead them home!' He said.

'I am the God of Abraham;
my name is I AM WHO I AM;
I'll get your race out of this jam –
to Canaan you'll be led!'

Or Yahweh.

Moses replied: 'They'll only laugh
if I say that!' 'Throw down your staff –

does that amaze your sight?' 'Not half!'
It was a snake instead...

'Proofs such as this will make them see
that you have my authority.'
'Fine – but my tongue lacks fluency.
I have an utter dread...

'...of public speaking!' 'Don't despair.
Your brother Aaron will be there.
Your would-be words *he* will declare –
he'll know what's in your head!'

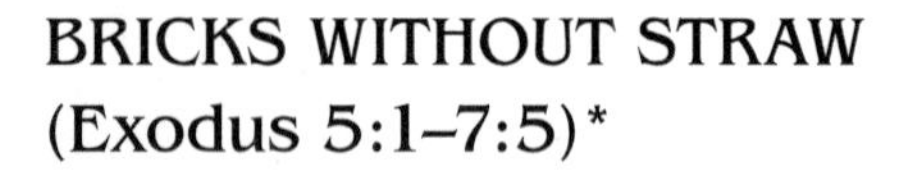

BRICKS WITHOUT STRAW (Exodus 5:1–7:5)*

* There are repetitions in the text, suggesting that different sources have been patched together. For example, 6:30 virtually repeats 6:12.

Their interview with Egypt's king
was not exactly promising...
'Our God will punish us, unless
we go into the wilderness
and worship Him. All right to go?'
Pharaoh, as you'd expect, said 'No,
it's not! I never heard such cheek!
For that, you'll work more hours per week
than you have ever worked before!
Since making bricks requires straw,
I've had you furnished with the stuff;
but from now on, to get enough,
you're going to have to glean the stubble –
you'll be too knackered to make trouble!'
The Israelites were furious...
'You two have made things worse for us!
Our quota hasn't been reduced –
how can we get these bricks produced?'

'Lord, help your people!' Moses cried,
'and prove to them you're on their side!'
So God informed him of His plan
to sort out this unpleasant man...
'I'll make him carry on refusing,
till, at a moment of my choosing,
I'll smite his people. Then he'll know
I'm to be feared, and you should go.
I have prepared some graded threats.'
Which one will clinch it? Place your bets!

THE FIRST NINE PLAGUES OF EGYPT: Exodus 7:14–10:29

1. The Plague of Blood (7:14–24)

'Tell Pharaoh: "I will curse the Nile
and turn its streams to blood.
The odour will be pretty vile
as fish rot in the mud!"'
The land stank with a vengeance. Phew!
But Pharaoh's wizards cursed it too.
'Is that the worst your God can do?
I'd give Him up, if I were you!'
said Pharaoh, unimpressed; and so
he wouldn't let them go...

2. The Plague of Frogs (7:25–8:15)

'Frogs will engulf you,' Moses said.
'You'll find them everywhere...
In ovens, kneading troughs, your bed,
and even in your hair!'
'That's no great trick,' Pharaoh replied;
'but make the pestilence subside,
and I will set you free!' He lied...

Although the frogs declined and died,
God hardened Pharaoh's heart, and so
he wouldn't let them go.

3. The Plague of Gnats (8:16–19)

Aaron was told to use his rod
to raise a cloud of dust.
The power of the Hebrew God
left Pharaoh's lot nonplussed.
'Look – every speck's become a gnat!
How can He do a trick like that?
They're ruining our habitat!'
'I will not let them leave – that's flat!'
hard-hearted Pharaoh said, and so
they weren't allowed to go.

4. The Plague of Flies (8:20–32)

God said to Moses: 'Tell the king
that Flies are shortly due.
They'll crawl around on everything,
and that's including you!
But where my people live, there'll be
a no-fly zone, as you will see!'
Although he made the king agree
to offer them an amnesty,
God hardened Pharaoh's heart, and so
not one of them could go.

5. The Plague of Livestock (9:1–7)

'Your livestock will be struck by plague,'
Moses was told to say.
The details are somewhat vague –
they all died anyway,
though not a goat or sheep or horse

the Hebrews owned was touched, of course!
These people were a vital source
of Pharaoh's massive labour force;
and to maintain the status quo
he simply wouldn't let them go.

6. The Plague of Boils (9:8–12)

'Take soot in handfuls from a flue
and throw it high before the king.
The people's skin (their livestock's too)
will straight away start festering.'
Moses obeyed the ordination...
The agonizing encrustation
quite paralysed the population,
but Pharaoh scorned negotiation
since God controlled his mind; and so
he wouldn't let them go.

7. The Plague of Hail (9:13–35)

'Tell Pharaoh: "I have held my hand –
you could have been eliminated!
Tomorrow, Egypt's mighty land
is going to be inundated
with Hail!"' This catastrophe
beat down the crops, stripped every tree...
'Oh, please stop doing this to me!'
cried Pharaoh, 'take your liberty!'
But God made him backslide, and so
they weren't allowed to go.

8. The Plague of Locusts (10:1–20)

When Moses threatened Locusts too,
the king's advisers said:
'Release them – that's what you *must* do,

or else we'll all be dead!'
He wouldn't soften in the least...
The locusts swarmed in from the east,
and Pharaoh said: 'Once this has ceased,
I'll have the Israelites released!'
The locusts left, but even so
he changed his mind, and still said 'No!'

9. The Plague of Darkness (10:21–29)

The Lord told Moses: 'Stretch your hand
towards the sky – that's right!
Darkness will smother Pharaoh's land,
but you will live in light.'
For three days, Egypt was benighted,
and Moses found himself invited
to meet the king... 'I'd be delighted
to have your passage expedited!'
said Pharaoh: 'Off you go –
but you must leave your flocks behind.'
'We'll take them too, if you don't mind,'
said Moses, 'since I'm not inclined
to higgle-haggle with your kind –
that is my *quid pro quo*!'

THE TENTH PLAGUE AND THE PASSOVER: 11:1–12:30

God said to Moses: 'Now the scene is set!
Nine times in all I've hardened Pharaoh's heart.
Tonight will be a night he won't forget...
He'll *plead* with you to pack up and depart!

'Ask your Egyptian neighbours to supply
whatever gold and silver they don't need

[the Hebrews' popularity was high,
and Moses' rating very good indeed].

'And then tell Pharaoh: "This will be the night
when every household weeps over its dead.
At midnight (more or less) the Lord will smite
each first-born male – man and quadruped.

'"The holocaust will spare neither your son
nor first-born children of the lowliest slave.
Each family will be reduced by one –
but all the Hebrews and their flocks He'll save."

'Then tell your people: "Kill the male lambs,
and cook them with the herbs you have prepared.
Your doorframe (both the lintel and the jambs)
daub with their blood – those dwellings will be spared...

'"...for when the Angels of the Lord draw near,
they'll see the blood, and leave the house alone.
You'll give thanks for my favour every year
at *Passover,* as this night shall be known!"'

Despite the gold and silver they'd donated,
every Egyptian household woke and wept.
Their first-born sons had been exterminated.
The fearful promise of the Lord was kept...

THE ESCAPE: Exodus 12:31–14:31

1. Night flight (12:31–14:8)

When Pharaoh woke to sounds of wailing,
and saw his threats were unavailing,
he told the brothers: 'That's enough!
Leave Egypt, please, with all your stuff –
but bless me first, before you go!'
The Hebrews packed unleavened dough
(there wasn't time to add the yeast)
and headed, it is thought, south-east,
instead of going straight away
to Canaan. This involved delay
(some forty years), but it is stated*
that till they had recuperated
and regained some *esprit de corps*,
it would be mad to fight a war
against the Philistines, whose land
edged Canaan. God's gigantic band –
six hundred thousand men approx.,
(in all, two million, plus their flocks)
followed the pillar in the sky
that God had sent to guide them by
(a cloud by day, by night a fire).
The Lord still harboured a desire
to show the Pharaoh who was boss,
despite the latter's crushing loss,
and so He made the chosen race
wander around from place to place
as though they couldn't navigate.
Pharaoh could not resist the bait:
'Why did we let them all go free?
They propped up our economy!
Assemble all the troops we've got,
and harness every chariot!'

* Ex 13:17.

2. Which sea did they cross?

Historiographers dispute
the Israelites' immortal route
and where the tidal wave occurred.
The Bible has the Hebrew word
Yam-Suf, which means the Weedy Sea* –
but which 'sea' is a mystery.
If Pharaoh followed helter-skelter,
a salt lake in the Nile Delta
could be where they were overtaken.
Tradition, though, will not be shaken:
of all the sites that suit the name,
the Red Sea has the hallowed claim…

* Or Sea of Reeds.

3. Tsunami (14:9–31)

The Israelites gave out a howl
and virtually threw in the towel
when Pharaoh's chariots appeared.
'This is *exactly* what we feared!'
they moaned to Moses; 'if we'd stayed,
we'd be all right!' 'Be not afraid,'
he told them, 'God will sort things out –
just wait and see!' 'Don't hang about!'
thundered the Lord, 'make for Yam-Suf,
where you'll be offered further proof
of what the Lord your God can do!
Between their chariots and you
my useful pillar will divide
the light and dark – night on their side,
and day on yours! I'll raise a breeze
(stretch out your staff to start it, please)
that drives a passage through the sea –
your alleyway to liberty!'
The east wind roared: the waters parted,
and God told Moses: 'Right – get started!'

The riven waters formed a wall
and nobody got wet at all;
but now the chariots give chase...
The distance shrinks with every pace...
The Israelites cannot go faster...
The whole thing's a complete disaster...
Then, as they urge their horses on,
the drivers find their wheels have gone –
as mentioned in Verse 25,

such chariots are hard to drive.*
The hold-up lets the fleeing band
outstrip their foes, and reach dry land.
'Stretch out your staff over the sea,
and that will fix them properly!'
the Lord tells Moses, once they've crossed –
and all of Pharaoh's host are lost.

* Some versions state that God merely jammed their wheels.

SURVIVAL: 15:22–17:7

The Israelites complain and fuss
throughout the whole of Exodus,
shaky of faith, quickly depressed,
and making out that life was best
in Egypt. 'It was your idea
to lead us on, and bring us here,'
they tell the harassed Moses. 'Why?

Far better to be slaves than die!'
Faced with this seething discontent,
it was on God that Moses leant...
The Lord gave him a piece of wood
that made a bitter spring taste good;
and in the second month, He said:
'Tonight eat meat; tomorrow, bread!'
On cue a flock of quail appeared,
consenting to be plucked and speared
on skewers, for their evening roast;
but what is now remembered most
is something that their Menu Planner
provided every morning: *Manna*!*
It lay around the camp like dew –
one 'omer' saw an adult through
(about 2 litres, it is thought).

15:23–25.

16:11–36.

* The solidified sap of certain desert plants, notably the tamarisk.

Its shelf life, though, was rather short;
if not consumed during the day,
the rest had to be thrown away.
Through forty years of life in tents,
their dietary requirements

were met by this amazing stuff...
But even this was not enough –
whenever things got tough, they moaned.
Once Moses cried: 'I shall be stoned
if we don't find some H_2O –
please help me, Lord!' The rest you know...
God told him: 'Give that rock a whack –

17:5–7.

if I were you, I'd stand well back!'*
Out of the stone the water poured,
and faith was (fleetingly) restored...

* The name of the place where this occurred is given as Mount Horeb. But Deut 5:2 suggests that Mount Horeb is where the Covenant was made.

UP THE MOUNTAIN: Exodus 19

Three months* after that fatal day
when Pharaoh's firstborn passed away,
they reached the Sinai Wilderness.
It is an educated guess
(though other places fit the bill)
that Jebel Musa (Moses Hill)
is where the Chosen Race first heard
the Voice of God... He had conferred
with Moses, keeping out of sight,

* The Hebrew calendar was, and still is, based on the lunar month.

upon the mountain's quaking height –
a good 6 on the Richter Scale.
'Upon the third day, without fail,
they must assemble, smartly dressed.
Before this happens, have them blessed
and in a proper state of grace.
Stand them around the mountain's base,
but if they dare to come too near,
stone them, or kill them with a spear.
I'm going to offer them a deal
along these lines (say what you feel):
Obey my rules and regulations,
and you'll be first among the nations!'
So Moses promised to report
exactly what the others thought,
and met the elders for a chat.
They said: 'We'll go along with that!'
The Day of Days arrived at last.
It started with a trumpet blast...

THE TEN COMMANDMENTS: Exodus 20:1–17

Out of the tumult and the smoke,
the people heard the words God spoke...

'The First Law that I'll set in stone
reads *Worship me, and me alone!*
The next says Idols are profane;
the Third, don't take my Name in vain;
the Fourth says keep the Seventh Day free;
the Fifth, treat Parents properly;
the Sixth says Murdering is wrong
(you knew the Seventh all along);*.

* Do not commit adultery.

the Eighth is crystal clear on Thieving,
as is the Ninth, on Not Deceiving;
and now the last of all my laws –
don't Covet things that are not yours.
So now you've learned them off by heart,
obey them – that's the tricky part!'

MORE RULES AND REGULATIONS: Exodus 20–31 overall

That wasn't all He said that day;*
the list of laws they must obey
(for instance, banning Usury)
extends to Chapter 23!
He then explained what must be done
(see 25–31)
to make a Tent* in which to store
the Tablets of the Written Law,
which He would very soon supply
(these precious stones must always lie
within the Ark – a wooden chest).
He said how priests ought to be dressed,
and what they are supposed to do;
altars and ephods,* lamp stands too,
and other vital ritual gear
are mentioned in great detail here,
as well as how a ram is bled –
the works, in fact, from A to Z!
Once Moses knew all this by heart,
and he was ready to depart,
the Lord put in his nervous grip
the Tablets of the Fellowship...

* The ancient scribes were not always concerned with sequential reporting. The Giving of the Laws may not have been the single event reported here.

* The Tabernacle.

* Priestly outer garment.

THE GOLDEN CALF: Exodus 32

Now Aaron did a dreadful thing
while Brother was aloft...
He told the Israelites to bring
their gold (such as an earring),
which they would kindly let him fling
into a fire. When soft...

...he carved a Calf most skilfully
(which broke the Second Law*).
They worshipped it devotedly,
indulged in wanton revelry,
and were as happy as could be!
God gawped at what He saw...

...and said to Moses: 'What a crew!
The whole thing's a disgrace!
You leave them, and that's what they do!
Well, now they've gone too far – I'm through!
I'll wipe them out, and trust in *you*
to start the Chosen Race!'

'Oh Lord,' cried Moses, 'stay your hand!
Reflect before you act!
Your anger I can understand;
but you agreed to bring this band
from Exile to the Promised Land –
you made a solemn pact!'

'All right – though I'd prefer *your* genes!
Got all the Laws? Take care!'
When Moses heard the tambourines

* Idols are profane.

and witnessed the licentious scenes,
he smashed the stones to smithereens –
past all hope of repair!

And then he wrecked the Calf, and cried:
'Who's with me, for the Lord?'
The Levites rallied to his side,
and with his orders they complied –
3,000 of their fellows died
as though God swung the sword...

'The Lord,' said Moses, 'was impressed
to see you kill your own.
The tribe of Levi will be blessed.*
I've no idea about the rest –
I'll mediate and do my best.
Lord God, let me atone...

* They became the priestly tribe, with special privileges.

'...for all their sins. Heap on my head
the crimes that they have done.'
'That wouldn't help at all!' He said.
'Without you, how would they be led?
I'll hit them with a plague instead,
to show who's No. 1!'

GETTING THERE: Exodus–Numbers

The stones he'd smashed beyond repair
required a replacement pair,
on which God wrote the Laws again –
a copy of the previous Ten.

Ex 34:1.

Then Moses laid them both to rest

within the Ark, or sacred chest,
that Bezalel, an artisan,
made to the Lord's specific plan.

Ex 37:1–9.

It stood within the holiest place
(the Tabernacle's curtained space)
when they were camped; but when *en route*
it led them, and they followed suit.
The Israelites were not allowed
to march, if God had cast a cloud
over the Tent; till it was clear,
they had to wait (up to a year!)
until it lifted, come what may.
And so they started on their way...
Their route was by no means direct;
on reaching Edom, they were checked
by Jacob's brother Esau's kin,

Num 20:14–21.

refused a fight they couldn't win
without the Lord's uncertain backing,
and did some tedious side-tracking

east of the Dead Sea. Major fights
with Sihon and his Amorites
and with the Bashan king (called Og)
were just two in a catalogue
of highly motivated slaughter.
(Cozbi, a Midianite's daughter,
seduced an Israelite. For this,
Moses decreed a nemesis:
'Kill everyone, the women too –
the virgins I'll reserve for you.')
So forty busy years went past,
till Jordan's stream was reached at last...

Num 21:21–35.

Num 31:1–18.

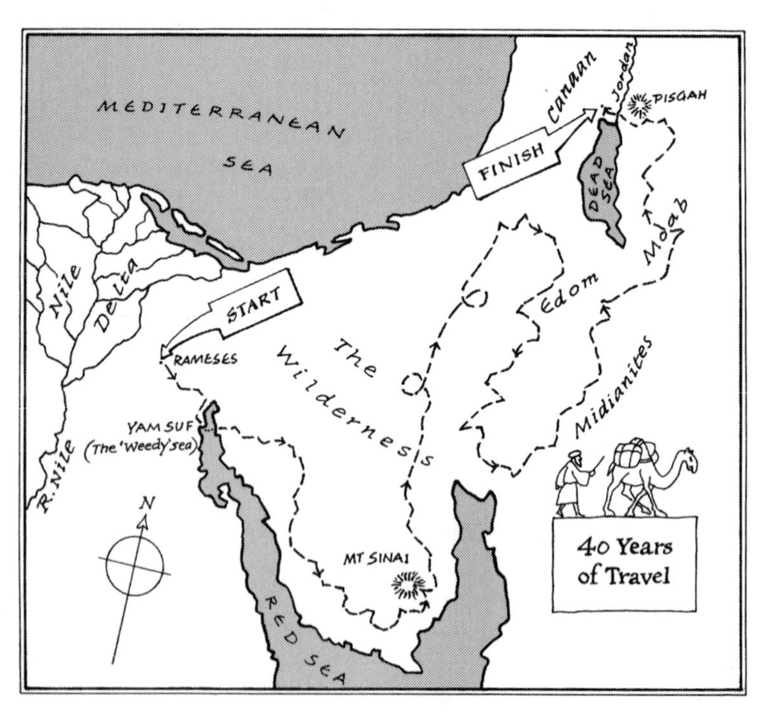

TROUBLE AHEAD:
Deuteronomy 31:14–32:43

The Lord told Moses: 'Sing this song...
Get all the Israelites along,
and make them learn it. Then they'll see
I prophesied their perfidy!'

The Valedictory Song of Moses

The Lord is great – He can do nothing wrong!
Oh, why did you reject Him out of hand?
He kept his bargain with you all along,
and brought you safely to the Promised Land...

The apple of His eye, you used to be!
Beneath His eagle's wings you were protected.
The Promised Land was shared out equably;
but you grew lazy, fat and disaffected!

Soon you forgot the One who brought you here,
forgot your bargain, gave Him no more thought...
He's somebody you really ought to fear –
His blade is keen, His temper very short!

Tergiversators!* You must take the blame
for calling forth the anger of the Lord!
He speaks now: '*Jealous* is my middle name,
in blood is *Vengeance* etched upon my sword!

'The Canaanites' false gods led you astray,
and on your heads my wrathful fire will fall.
For this contempt, both young and old will pay,
until there is no Chosen Race at all...

* Backsliders.

'Forbear, my sword; my jealous rage, abate!
If I kill them, how will my status seem?
The heathen Canaanites will celebrate –
their idols will appear to reign supreme!

'No – they will suffer, but avoid defeat...
The gods they turned to, they will then despise;
and when their foes' destruction is complete,
how great will be my stature in their eyes!'

Thus, Moses' song concluded on a high,
despite the cataclysms on the way...
He'd seen the Land, and it was time to die;
but where he's buried, nobody can say.

CHAPTER 4

CARVING UP CANAAN (Joshua–Judges)

THE LIEUTENANT: Numbers 27:12–23

From time to time we've heard the sound
of *Joshua*. He is around
to lead one of their earliest fights,
which wipes out the Amalekites;*
and he's with Moses when they see
the Golden Calf debauchery
(if Josh had climbed the mountain too,
then he was special, in God's view).
Well, when their trek was at an end,
God said to Moses: 'I intend
to put you on a nice high spot
facing the Land – but that's your lot!
You doubted me, as I recall,
before I made the water fall
out of the rock at Meribah.*
I said I'd let you walk this far,
but I would never let you tread
on Canaan's acres!' Moses said
(as he enjoyed the splendid view
from Pisgah's summit*): 'That's quite true!

* Ex 17:8–16.

* The Water from the Rock episode appears again at Num 20:1-13, when Moses is told that he won't reach the Promised Land because he showed lack of faith.

* Deut 34:1.

But somebody will have to keep
a watchful eye on all these sheep,
or they will simply cut and run!'
'Choose Joshua, the son of Nun,
a man in whom the Spirit blazes,
to lead them through the early phases...'

RITES OF PASSAGE: Joshua 3–5:9

On Jordan's brink, the stage was set...
To stop their feet from getting wet,
God held the flowing waters back,
and in the middle of the track
the Levites held the Ark on high
while 40,000 men marched by –
all armed. Then came a painful pause...
Despite the circumcision laws,
no infant children had been treated
since Egypt's army was defeated!
Josh therefore ordered every male
to join the line-up without fail,
before his trumpets (as you know!)
blew down the walls of Jericho...

SAVING RAHAB: Joshua 2 and 6

The walls of Jericho were wide,
and on the top (or else inside)
a whore named Rahab sold her wares.
Two spies from Josh climbed up the stairs
and found her most accommodating.
'Don't worry, dears! The whole land's waiting
in what I might call *trepidation*.
You've earned yourselves a reputation,

what with the way you sorted out
Kings Og and Sihon!* How about
a deal between your chief and me?
I've talked, so save my family!'
She lowered a rope; they both descended,
and told Josh it was undefended.
Six days his army marched around
the ramparts, to their trumpets' sound;
but on the seventh, the procession
did seven circuits in succession –
then, with an ear-splitting blast,
they cried: 'The city's ours at last!'
The walls fell down, and in they poured...
No living thing was spared the sword,
although, as Rahab stipulated,
she and her kin were relocated.
Josh spoke this curse: 'Whoever tries
to raise this city where it lies
will lose his firstborn – and his least.' *
His stature rapidly increased...

* Num 21:21–35.

* Youngest.

AI – A CASE STUDY: Joshua 7–8

Throughout their tenure of the land,
the Israelites were underhand –
the Lord's commands were disobeyed,
or, even worse, devotion strayed
to other gods. Anger would burn
within the Lord... 'You'll never learn!
You're wilful, faithless and obtuse –
I'll let you stew in your own juice!'
And so He would, but then they'd cry
'Forgive us, Lord!' The case of Ai
(to which I shall devote this section)
shows God's procedure to perfection...

All this was predicted in the Song of Moses.

1. The sin (7:1)

When Jericho had been laid waste,
the treasure it contained was placed
before the Lord – these fruits of war
were His and His alone, by law!
But somebody in Judah's army
(his name was Achan, son of Carmi)
decided he would keep a bit –
and everybody paid for it...

2. The punishment (7:2–5)

Ai was a city in their way,
but Josh's spies came back to say
that it would be a cinch to take:
'Three thousand men – a piece of cake!'
However, they were put to flight...
Three dozen* perished in the fight,
and when the rest got back to base,
bewildered Josh fell on his face.
'Oh Lord, if news of this should spread,
we're finished! We're as good as dead!'

* It doesn't sound many, but it showed that God had forsaken them.

3. The atonement (7:10–26)

'Get up!' the Lord said. 'Can't you see
it's Israelite mendacity
that made the battle turn out so?
Someone removed from Jericho
part of the plunder that is mine.
Tell everyone to stand in line...
I'll help you choose the tribe, the clan,
the unit – and the guilty man!'
Soon Joshua had made his choice,
inspired by that inner voice –
the tribe of Judah was selected,

the fruits of Carmi's loins inspected,
and Achan was identified.
'It's in my tent!' the sinner cried.
They stoned him and his kinsfolk too,
which was the proper thing to do.

4. The reconciliation (8:1–29)

The Lord told Joshua: 'All right –
you're once more favoured in my sight,
so let me act as your adviser.
To take Ai, it would be much wiser
to set an ambush for their men
and kill them. Go and try again!'
They sworded all the population,
started a massive conflagration,
and hanged the king upon a tree
for showing such hostility.

JOSHUA OUTSMARTED: Joshua 9

Of Joshua it may be said,
no leader left more people dead!
God made his job description clear:
Destroy the kingdoms that are here,
achieve a stable situation,
and give each tribe its allocation.
(The Lord used His Egyptian ruse –
He made the kings refuse a truce,
which meant they *had* to be attacked,
their subjects slain, their cities sacked.)
Thirty-one kingdoms were destroyed,
but Joshua was most annoyed
when Gibeon, the thirty-second,
escaped his sword. Its leaders reckoned

11:20.

Listed at 12:7–24.

that if a treaty could be signed
(however falsely), it would bind
the Israelites to non-aggression...
One day, a pitiful procession
arrived at Joshua's HQ –
their wineskins cracked, their shoes worn through,
their bread hard, dry, and green with mould.
'We've come far,' Joshua was told,
'our journey's taken many a day;
but though we live so far away
(beyond your sphere of influence)
we thought it might, perhaps, make sense
to reach some non-aggression deal.'
Josh, taken in by their appeal,
swore peace before the penny fell –
they lived near by, they'd lied like hell;*
he'd been egregiously tricked!
However, oaths were very strict,
and even when induced by fraud,
to break them would annoy the Lord.
(Recall how Isaac had been caught
by blessing Esau, as he thought,
though it was Jacob in disguise.*)
'Mendacious churls! Your country lies
within the Promised Land,' he said.
'But for my oath, you'd all be dead.
Hew wood, fetch water – from now on
that is the role of Gibeon!'

* An anachronism. Hell (and indeed afterlife) were not concepts known to the Israelites.

* Gen 27.

THE CARVE-UP:
Joshua 13–Judges 1

The great Lieutenant's power was waning...
The Lord said: 'Thanks to your campaigning
the Israelites have got their hands
on some of the allotted lands,
though there are still large tracts to seize.
It's time you allocated these,
making it clear which tribe owns what
(whether they've won the land or not).'*
Chapters 13–21
set out the share for everyone,
and this map shows the land they had,
though Reuben, Manasseh and Gad
already owned exclusive rights
to land won in the earlier fights
east of the Jordan. Manasseh*
became two 'half-tribes', by the way,

* The tribe of Dan did not come into their inheritance until after the time of Samson (Judg 18:1).

* Joseph's eldest son.

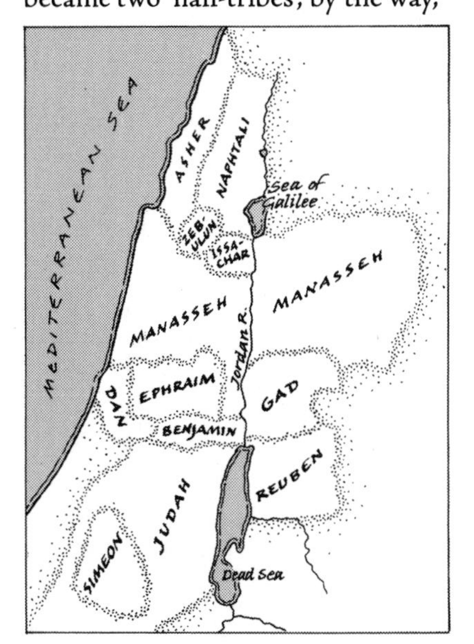

and as the map shows, they possessed
more land than any of the rest...

Joshua 24.

At Shechem, with a three-line whip,
Josh looked back on his stewardship,
and told them all: 'I'll soon be gone;
but God will help you carry on
and win the lands that still await.
Now listen... *Never* integrate
with those you conquer. If you do,
and their gods get their hooks in you,
the Lord won't like it – once you swerve,
you'll get the fate that you deserve.'

*

So farewell to the son of Nun,
who battled on, and always won...
The Lord told Judah: 'Now he's dead,
you'll be my right-hand tribe instead,
so conquer the remaining land –
I'll offer you a helping hand!'*
(One of the cities seized by them
turns out to be Jerusalem.)
Not every single Canaanite
was massacred, or put to flight;
but they were re-employed as drudges...
And now we've reached the Book of Judges,
when things go seriously wrong –
as Moses foresaw in his Song!

* The Lord deliberately left some Canaanite kingdoms intact, in order to test the Israelites (Judg 2:20–23).

CHAPTER 5

RULED BY THE JUDGES (Judges)

LED BY A WOMAN: Judges 2:10–4:24

The generation passed away
that Joshua had led.
Their progeny would go astray,
preferring gods like Baal, say,
or Asherah, instead.*
God saw it all, and shook His head...

* Male and female deities of Babylonian origin. The word 'Baal' prefixes a number of different gods, for example 'Baal-Berith' (8:32).

'I left, as part of my design,
some kingdoms here and there
(both Canaanite and Philistine)*
to wage war on this race of mine
if they should vacillate, and dare
to worship deities elsewhere...

* 'Canaanite' is loosely applied to all indigenous tribes west of the Jordan. The Philistines were originally a Mediterranean people who settled in the coastal regions nearer Egypt.

'As if that wasn't bad enough,
they've scorned the rule I made,
and married bits of foreign fluff!
They may believe they've called my bluff;
but since our pact has been betrayed,
they'll do without me, I'm afraid!'

But as it says in Judges 2,
whenever threats occurred,
the Lord thought: 'What I'd better do
is send a Judge to pull them through!'
(Although 'Judge' is the written word,
'Leader' is much to be preferred.)

So, every time they were attacked,
they'd turn to Him, and plead:
'We need a Judge, and that's a fact!
We're very sorry we backtracked!
Please help us in our urgent need –
we'll worship you if we succeed!'

The name of *Deborah* you'll know –
a Judge who had been sent
to sort out Sisera,* their foe.
But Jael struck the final blow
when Sisera unwisely went
to shelter in her husband's tent...

* A Canaanite commander.

He had been licked, and put to flight.
'I wouldn't mind a drink,' he said.
'I've got some milk, if that's all right!'
said Jael. Tired from the fight,
he let her tuck him up in bed
and bang a tent peg through his head.

THE SONG OF DEBORAH: Judges 5

With a grateful nod to Alfred, Lord Tennyson: 'The Charge of the Light Brigade'.

God was your Guide and Might,
Canaan had come in sight,
Cloud by day, fire by night –
Onward you thundered!

Swords into ploughshares beat,
Organic crops to eat –
Canaan was honey-sweet!
That's when you blundered...

Worshipped false gods of theirs,
Engendered doubtful heirs,
Had a great time – who cares?
God's links were sundered!
Canaanites drawing near,
People cry out in fear:
'Deborah – need you, dear!
We're being plundered!'

'All right,' I say, 'I'll go!'
Fighting near Megiddo...*
Slay the entire foe!
Sisera's blundered!
Jael soon picks his brain,
Everything's right as rain...
But they'll soon stray again,
In case you wondered!

* Said to be the Armageddon of tradition, and the site of an important British victory over the Ottoman Turks during the First World War.

GIDEON, UNCROWNED KING: Judges 6–8

1. Baal-Basher (6:1–32)

To curb the strength of Midian*
God fast-tracked humble Gideon,
Joash's son. 'Stop threshing wheat,'
an Angel said, 'You need to beat
your enemies. God's on your side!'
'He can't be,' Gideon replied.
'If He was here, as you suggest,
He'd never let us be oppressed!

* An Arabian tribe.

Oh, by the way, I'd like to see
some proof of your identity –
not that I'm saying you're a liar!'
The Angel set a rock on fire,
and gobsmacked Gideon awaited
his orders from the Lord, which stated:
'My wish is this – that without fail
you wreck your father's shrine to Baal,
and burn the pole he raised nearby
to Asherah.' The hue and cry
reached Joash... 'Hand over your son –
he's going to die for what he's done!'
But Joash said: 'That makes no sense!
These gods should fight in self-defence –
my lad's destroyed them, fair and square!'
They all agreed, and then and there
dubbed Gideon the 'Baal-Basher'.*
The tribes of Manasseh and Asher
and Zebulun (Naphtali too)
heard of his fame. Let's start Part 2...

* A loose translation of the Hebrew 'Jerub-Baal'.

2. Fixing the odds (7:1–8:21)

Those four tribes clamoured to his call –
32,000 came in all.
'It's overkill!' the Lord complained,
'with these, your triumph will be gained
without the slightest help from me –
so where's my credibility?
Reduce them, and increase the odds,
to prove the victory is God's!'
Our hero cried out: 'Who's afraid?
Right – go back home!' Ten thousand stayed,
but God was far from satisfied.
'Tell them to drink, and then decide...
The ones who make their hands a cup

to lap the river water up,
you will select for your elite.'
Three hundred men drank on their feet
instead of lying on their faces,
and took up their allotted places
in three small companies, which crept
to where the Midianites slept.
Each had a torch inside a pot
(which must have got extremely hot),
and held a trumpet, which he blew
when Baal-Basher told him to,
shouting: 'For God and Gideon!'
They smashed their pots: their torches shone
upon disoriented foes
exchanging devastating blows;
and as you'll probably have guessed,
they quickly sorted out the rest.

3. Meltdown (8:22–9:57)

The people cried: 'Rule over us!'
'No way! The Lord's victorious,
not I – He is your only king!
Just let me have an earring
out of the booty you have seized.'
The Lord must have been most displeased
to see him melt the metal down
and mould a golden priestly gown
(an ephod), which they bowed before –
an insult to the Second Law!*
When Gideon declined and died
his wives had left him well supplied
with seventy sons; the seventy-first,
Abimelech (by far the worst)
was borne him by his concubine.
To make sure he was first in line,

* Idols are profane.

his brothers got it in the neck,
and horrible Abimelech
enjoyed three years of bloody power
before a woman in a tower
let fall a millstone on his head.
'She's cracked my skull!' the tyrant said,
'so run me through immediately –
no woman gets the best of me!'

SAMSON THE STRONG: Judges 13–16

The leaders identified in the Book of Judges are as follows:

Othniel (3:9)
Ehud (3:15)
Shamgar (3:31)
Deborah (4:4)
Gideon (6:11)
Abimelech (8:31)
Tola (10:1)
Jair (10:3)
Jephthah (11:1)
Ibzan (12:8)
Elon (12:11)
Abdon (12:13)
Samson (13:24)

The references are to their first mention.

With thirteen Judges in the list
(and no doubt others have been missed),
I've only room to rhyme one more –
the fellow you've been waiting for...

1. Guerrilla fighter (13–15)

Manoah's wife, who had been child-free,
received an unexpected Visitation.
An Angel said: 'If you eat sensibly
and keep off drink produced by fermentation...

'the Lord will bless you, and a son you'll bear,
who's set apart by God – a *Nazirite*.*
Remember now – you mustn't cut his hair.
He's going to be a mighty Israelite!'

The Philistines had overrun the land.
Young Samson grew up in a subject race,
but when he came of age, he sought the hand
of one of *them*. He went down to her place...

* Nazirites were a recognized class, sanctified to God from birth. Not to be confused with Jesus's label of *Nazarene* – a resident of Nazareth.

...disposing of a lion on the way.
They plighted, though his parents were distressed.
Then, when he went back on his wedding day,
inside the beast some bees had made their nest.

He told her kinsmen: 'If you can complete
a riddle that I've managed to devise
(i.e., *Out of the strong came something sweet*),
you stand to win a super-duper prize...

'...but if you can't, the prize will come to me!'
They told her: 'Find the answer out for us.'
She wormed it out of him eventually,
and so they won. Was Samson furious!

When they snatched back his wife, the war began...
Incendiary foxes were deployed,
with flares tied to their tails. Off they ran!
The Philistines, exceedingly annoyed...

...at having all their crops incinerated,
chased after him, so Samson went and hid.
His antics made his kinsmen irritated –
'We're going to hand you over!' Which they did.

But at this point his lashings snapped like thread.
He seized the jawbone of an ass, and swung...
A thousand Philistines were laid out dead,
and Samson's virtues started to be sung...

Eyeless in Gaza: 16*

* 'Eyeless in Gaza at the mill with slaves, Himself in bonds under Philistian yoke.'
John Milton: *Samson Agonistes.*

Though physically he was very strong,
by pretty ladies he was quickly smitten;
when dazzling *Delilah* came along,
this Tarzan was as helpless as a kitten.

It was a put-up job. She stood to earn
a tidy sum, if she would use her arts
and help the frantic Philistines to learn
the secret of his strength. The story starts...

...within her bedroom. After teasing sessions,
Samson confides the secret of his strength –
his hair! (This most important of possessions
must be at least of floor-to-shoulder length.)

When he awakes, imagine his surprise –
she's turned *coiffeuse*, his tresses have been shorn!
The grateful Philistines gouge out his eyes,
and, safe in Gaza, get him grinding corn...

The people want to see him on display,
so in the temple they arrange a show.
'I'll hold on to these pillars, if I may?'
By now, his new hair has begun to grow...

He prays for extra strength, and gives a shove.
The roof falls, squashing everybody flat.
Three thousand people, watching up above,
die with their captive too – and that is that!

CHAPTER 6

SAMUEL, RELUCTANT KINGMAKER (Ruth 1–1 Samuel 15)

DAVID'S GREAT-GRANDMOTHER: Ruth 1–4

The Book of Ruth is very short,
its people of a kindlier sort
than those we're used to in these pages!
Her odyssey is in two stages...

1

A deep domestic tragedy
shatters the widow Naomi.
In Moab,* where she's gone to stay,
her married sons have passed away.
Their widows (Ruth and Orphah) grieve,
and she decides she'd better leave.
'This is your land,' she says to them.
'I'm going back to Bethlehem,
but you stay – if you play it right,
you'll each attract a Moabite!'
Orphah agrees, but Ruth says: 'No!
Wherever you go, I will go –
your people I will share with you,
and your God will be my God too!'

* Moab was a country east of the Dead Sea, through which the Israelites passed under Moses.

2

In Bethlehem, a rich relation
named Boaz, shows consideration,
and lets Ruth glean the alien wheat

to give them both enough to eat.
Well, Naomi suspects the truth
(that he is rather keen on Ruth);
he woos her on the threshing-floor,
and by the end of Chapter 4
they've grown a new branch on the Tree
of David's genealogy.
Obed, their son, has Jesse next
(the links are set out in the text);
and Jesse will in turn beget
King David – but we're not there yet...

THE CALLING OF SAMUEL: 1 Samuel 1–3

There now ensued a dismal phase
that heralded their greatest days,
for in the dark before the dawn
the timely Samuel was born.
Eli was Judge, a worthy priest,
but not assertive in the least;
his two sons* were another factor –
no *virgo* could remain *intacta*
(despite their outward priestly function)
nor did they have the least compunction
in dining off the tenderest slices
of other people's sacrifices.
The Lord told Eli: 'Fancy letting
that pair eat what *I* should be getting!
Your heirs will die before their prime –
I'll choose a better Judge next time!'*

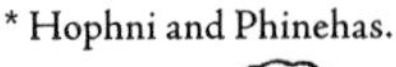
* Hophni and Phinehas.

*i.e., Samuel.

*

Now meet a certain lady, Hannah,
the wife of someone called Elkanah,

whose ecstasy made Eli think
she'd had a drop too much to drink.
She was, in fact, in voiceless prayer,
but as he watched her from his chair
and saw her tears and consternation
it did suggest inebriation.
However, when he censured her,
she told him: 'I'm quite sober, sir!
My words are for the Lord, who hears
beyond the range of human ears.
I'm childless! I want a son!'
Said Eli: 'May He send you one!'
So, having got the Judge to bless her,
Hannah gave birth to his successor...

*

When little Samuel* was born,
she took him to the Judge. 'I've sworn
that he will be the Lord's,' she said,
'no barber's blade will touch his head.'
Sam thus became a Nazirite,
and trained as Eli's acolyte...
One night, when sleeping by the Ark,*
the boy was woken by a 'Hark!'
and went to Eli. 'Did you call?'
'No, I did not!' Three times in all
the Judge was woken while he snored –
and then he guessed it was the Lord...
'Sam, if He calls again, just say:
"I hear you clearly – talk away!"
Now let me sleep!' The call came through,
and God said: 'I've some news for you.
I'm cutting off your master's line.
Henceforth he is no friend of mine.

* 'Samuel' may mean 'God heard him' in Hebrew.

* The Ark was still at Shiloh, where it had been since the time of Joshua.

His sons are rotten to the core –
he ought to have enforced the law!'
At breakfast, Eli asked him 'Well?'
and Samuel just had to tell.
The Judge sighed: 'Things have gone too far.
It's my fault – *que sera, sera!*'*

* What will be, will be.

FROM BAD TO WORSE: 1 Samuel 4:1–18

The Lord's wrath waxed exceeding strong
against the Judge, for doing wrong.
The Israelites went out and fought,
and ended up 4,000 short
when with the Philistines they battled.
This setback left the elders rattled.
'The Lord's deserted us!' they wailed.
A bold initiative prevailed –
the Ark would lead their next attack,
and when they'd won, they'd bring it back!
So it was taken from the Tent*
by Eli's sons, and off they went...
Oh, unimaginable woe!
Instead of scattering the foe,
the desperate device backfired –
the Philistines became inspired,
and at the most prodigious cost
the battle (and the Ark) were lost!

* Or Tabernacle.

Battle of Ebenezer.

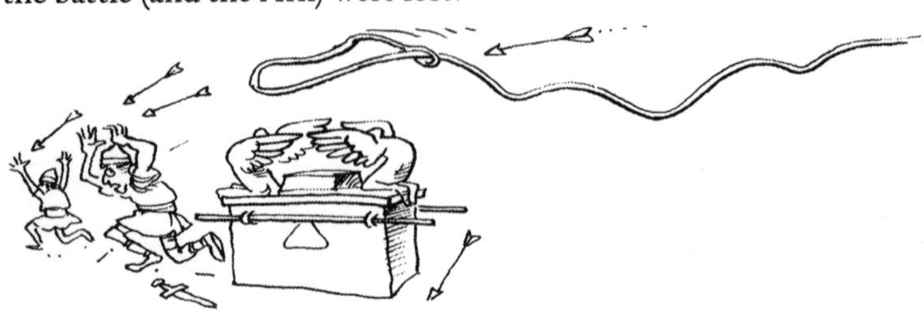

The Israelites gave up and fled,
leaving some 30,000 dead,
plus Eli's offspring. When he heard,
a curious event occurred –
the shock made him fall off his chair,
breaking his neck beyond repair,
since, as the book goes on to state,
the Judge was rather overweight.

TOXIC STUFF: 1 Samuel 5:1–7:2

The Philistines, of course, were thrilled
at all the Israelites they'd killed.
In Ashdod, victory complete,
the Ark was placed at Dagon's* feet,
but in the morning, when they rose,
he'd fallen forward on his nose!
They propped him up – again he fell,
and now his head came off as well.

* A harvest deity.

Contagion spread like wildfire,
the death-toll rising ever higher;
they therefore sent the Ark post-haste

(like dangerous atomic waste)
to Gath, where fatal tumours spread,
and so they passed it on instead
to Ekron, where the deadly thing
got everybody festering,
making them keen to lose it too.
The rulers wondered what to do,
and after pondering a bit,
decided to get rid of it.
'We'll pack it in a special cart,
hitch on two cows, and let them start
without a drover – if they go
towards the Israelites, we'll know
the Lord has managed these events;
if not, they were coincidence!'
The cows, continuously mooing,
began spontaneously pursuing
a path towards the opposition
at Beth-Shemesh. This apparition
amazed the populace, who saw
a sight unparalleled before –
the Ark returning on its own!
The Levites placed it on a stone,
the cart was smashed and set ablaze,
and in an outpouring of praise
the clever cows were barbecued.
But God was in a peevish mood –
He killed the seventy* who tried
to touch the Ark and peer inside,

* The Revised Version says 'seventy men and fifty thousand men'. The New International Version omits the fifty thousand.

and soon the residents implored
Abinadab to have it stored
inside his house.* And there it waited
for *David* to be consecrated...

* At Kearith Jearim.

KINGDOM COME? 1 Samuel 8

No other Judge did half as well
as soldier-statesman Samuel,
for under his enlightened reign
the Philistines collapsed again.
But as with Eli, so with Sam –
his two sons* didn't give a damn,
sold favours, and were widely felt
to be no good. The great man dwelt
at Ramah, where the elders went,
and told him: 'Both your sons are bent!
Our words to them are: "On your bike!"
A proper *king* is what we'd like –
someone to lead us into war.*
That's what a monarch should be for!'
Sam didn't share this point of view.
'Think of his power over you!
Your sons would fight for him, or plough
(you would have lost them, anyhow);
your daughters also would be his,
to soothe his nose with fragrances,
to bake his bread, or cook his meat –
and now I've mentioned things to eat,
one-tenth of everything you've grown,
as well as all the flocks you own,
a king would annex for his use.
You're being utterly obtuse!
After he's crowned, believe you me,

* Joel and Abijah.

* They were particularly afraid of Nahash, King of the Ammonites (12:12).

you will regret it bitterly!'
The elders, though, weren't listening,
and said again: 'Give us a king!'
The Lord, surprisingly, agreed:
'I think a king is what they need...'

SAUL CALLED: 1 Samuel 9–10

A man called Kish,* whose son (called Saul)
was quite exceptionally tall,
mislaid his donkeys. 'I'm afraid
the wretched animals have strayed,'
he told his son. 'Go off and see
if you can bring them back for me!'
The donkeys led Saul quite a dance,*
until, apparently by chance,
he reached a city miles away
where Samuel had gone to stay.
The Lord had briefed the Judge, who knew
the future king would be there too;
and when the giant came in sight,
God murmured: 'He's the one, all right!'
Sam blessed the oil in his flask,
and told Saul: 'It's a lot to ask,
but Israelites need to be led,
and you're the man!' Upon Saul's head
the sacramental juice was poured,
and Samuel explained: 'The Lord
is with you. Without even trying,
you'll find you've started prophesying!'

*

* A Benjamite.

* He never found them, but they fell into good hands and were returned.

At Mizpah, where the tribes collected,
Sam was downbeat. 'You have rejected
the Lord your God, who took your hand
and brought you to the Promised Land –
your comfort when you were distressed,
your sword and shield when oppressed!
A mortal king I don't advise –
however, try this one for size!'
He chose the tribe of Benjamin,
the clan of Matri, and the kin
of the Anointed's father, Kish...
But Saul himself, who didn't wish
to seem inordinately vain,
had hidden in the baggage train.
He dwarfed them all – a whole head higher!
What better king could they desire?

SAMUEL STILL DOWNBEAT: 1 Samuel 11–12

Saul's first and most successful fight,
against Nahash the Ammonite,
led to his formal coronation
before all Israel's population.
But Samuel would never budge
from his conviction that a Judge
(and not a king) would suit them best.
'God *is* your king, and here's a test –
I'll show you (*a*) what God can do,
and (*b*) that I've His ear too!'
They certainly began to wonder,
when Samuel called down rain and thunder
that flattened their ungarnered wheat...
Had they been rather indiscreet
in putting someone on the throne?

'You're right, Sam – we are God's alone!
Please do inform Him, from us all,
we're sorry we selected Saul!'
'Too late for that,' the Judge replied.
'God's basically on your side,
but if you ever start to stray,
He'll sweep you (and your king) away!'

SAUL REJECTED: 1 Samuel 13–15

The reign of Saul was problematic.
His judgement was at best erratic,
and God and Sam were soon regretting
their negligent approach to vetting...
At Micmash, Jonathan (Saul's son)
attacked some Philistines, and won;
but then the enemy assembled
a force so vast that it resembled
the grains of sand upon the shore.
Saul's soldiers didn't wait for more,
and fled. Sam blamed him for the mess...
'God would have crowned you with success
and let your dynasty succeed
if you had shown that you could lead;
but you did not, so He's selected
another leader.'* Though rejected,
Saul ruled till he was 72,*
a rather cheeky thing to do.

* i.e. David.

* The text says that he ruled for forty-two years, and he was thirty when crowned. However, we are told at 7:2 that the Ark remained at Kearith Jearim for only twenty years before David moved it to Jerusalem.

CHAPTER 7

SAUL v. DAVID
(1 Samuel 16–2 Samuel 4)

THE CHOOSING OF DAVID: 1 Samuel 16–17

David was due to follow Saul,
but there are three accounts in all
of how he's chosen from the rest.
I wonder which you like the best?

1st version: Samuel anoints David (16:1–13)

The Lord told Samuel: 'Fill up your flask.
Set off for Bethlehem – you've work to do!'
'Lord,' Samuel replied, 'what is my task?'
'Anoint a young man there – King No. 2!'

Sam went to Jesse's house (who, you'll recall,
was born to Ruth and Boaz earlier on),*
saw seven sons, and asked him: 'Are these all?'
'No – I've another. Where's young David gone?'

* Ruth 4:13–22.

The Lord said to His servant: 'This is he!'
So Sam anointed Jesse's youngest son
before his flabbergasted family,
then went back home. That's Version No. 1...

2nd version: The harpist (16:14–23)

God had cancelled His support.
Saul was feeling rather fraught.
Someone said: 'My lord, we thought
you might like a musician...

'...to play for you when you're distressed.
We feel a harpist might be best.'
(I daresay you've already guessed
who's primed for that position!)

So David, skimmer of the strings,
received this summons of the king's,
packed up some necessary things –
and passed the tough audition!

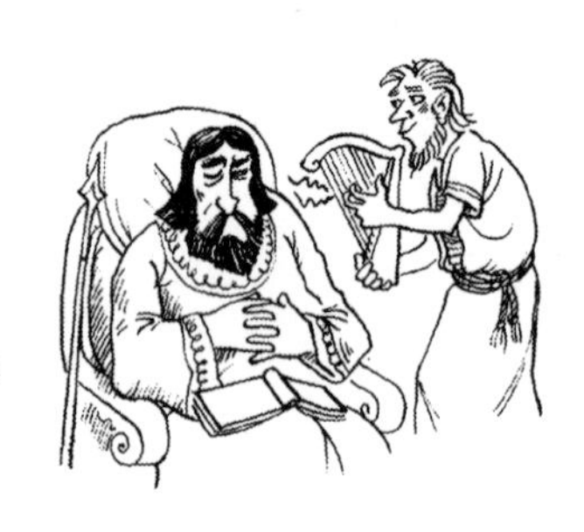

He was the one the king would choose
each time he suffered from the blues.
Young David helping Saul to snooze
is deep in our tradition...

3rd version: David and Goliath (17)

'Your brothers have gone off to fight,'
his father Jesse said.
'Please go and see if they're all right,
and take ten loaves of bread!'

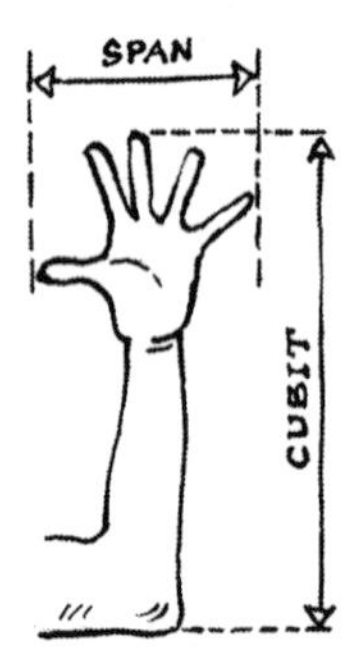

The troops stayed back behind their lines...
'What's wrong?' he asked a man.
'A giant's joined the Philistines –
six cubits and a span!*

* About three metres tall.

'This monster (called Goliath) cries:
"Whoever fights with me
and wins, wins all; but if he dies,
we claim the victory!"

'For forty days he's shouted thus,
but no one has replied.'
So David said: '*I'll* fight for us –
it's high time someone tried!'

'Prove you're the one, of all those here,
whom we can most rely on.'
'Well, though I didn't have a spear,
I massacred a lion!'

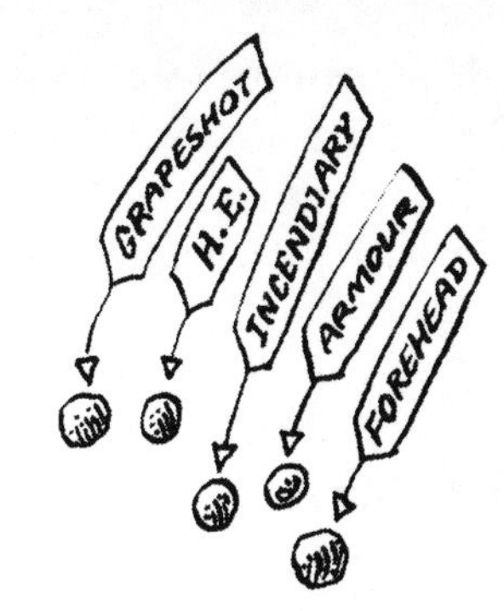

He earned the blessing of the king,
but armour he rejected:
his only weapon was a sling
and five stones he'd selected.

'I'll carve you up!' Goliath roared,
'the birds will be well-fed!'
But David slung his stone, and scored –
the giant fell down dead!

The Philistines were hacked to bits
(it was extremely messy),
and Saul, who suffered jealous fits,
despised the son of Jesse...

JOINING THE FAMILY: 1 Samuel 18

King Saul was chronically unstable
(there'll be some psychiatric label,
but God is meant to be behind
the monarch's topsy-turvy mind).
David, performing on his harp,
got used to being pulled up sharp
when Saul, upon a sudden whim,
took aim and hurled a spear at him.
The current hit at No. 1
praised Jesse's charismatic son –
a précis of the lyrics goes:
He's killed ten times as many foes

The 'evil spirits' that upset him were sent by God, because the concept of a Devil had no place in early Hebrew theology.

*as Saul has done!** This sort of thing
did not endear him to the king,
who came up with a cunning plan
to sort him out... 'You are the man
for Michal, my beloved daughter!
Just one proviso – you must slaughter
a hundred Philistines, to show
you're worthy of her. Off you go!'
Saul hoped he'd perish there and then,
and never bother him again,
but David left two hundred dead
(that's twice the number Saul had said).
The heap of foreskins proved the score –
he's now the royal son-in-law!

* 'Saul has slain his thousands, and David his ten thousands.' 1 Sam 18:7.

DAVID AND JONATHAN: 1 Samuel 18–20

His friendship with Saul's son and heir
has made them an 'iconic' pair
in Literature as well as Art.
In Chapter 18, near the start
(look at verse 3), it's plainly stated
that Jonathan's infatuated;
and Chapter 20, near the end,
shows David's feeling for his friend –
the two embrace (verse 41)
and down their cheeks the teardrops run,
though David is more lachrymose.
However, you should not suppose
that ladies don't affect him too –
Bathsheba will, I promise you!*

* 2 Sam 11.

THE OUTLAW: 1 Samuel 19:11–24:22

Michal, his wife, had chanced to hear
about a plot. 'You're wanted, dear!
My father's posted men outside,
so run away tonight and hide –
I'll plant a dummy in the bed,
and say you're ill!' Her husband fled
and turned into a refugee,
pursued by Saul relentlessly,
although their roles were twice reversed
when David spared him. Here's the first...
A Call of Nature brought the king
to where the band were sheltering
inside a cave... David crept near
and cut off, as a souvenir,
part of his robe, without King Saul
suspecting anything at all.
The monarch, once he'd finished pissing,
discovered that a piece was missing,*

* Poetic licence. Saul didn't know what David had done, until he told him.

and saw his son-in-law prostrated!
'My lord king, while you urinated

I did not strike, but let you pee –
I don't know why you're anti-me!
You are the king, and you I'll serve –
your wrath is more than I deserve!'
Saul made his usual *volte-face,*
and wept. 'I was an utter ass
to act in this aggressive way.
Let's call the whole thing off, OK?
So now we're friends!' They both embrace,
but David makes off, just in case...

DOUBLE AGENT: 1 Samuel 27

You'll find in Chapter 26
the second of these cheeky tricks,
when David found the monarch snoozing
and stole the spear that he was using...
Then, to escape King Saul's designs,
he went and joined the Philistines!
King Achish gave his men a town
called Ziklag, where they settled down
and raided cities which, in fact,
his master didn't want attacked,
since they were part of his domain!
He made sure everyone was slain,
for not a witness must there be
to whisper his duplicity.

THE FALL OF SAUL: 1 Samuel 28–31

'I plan to hit Saul very hard –
I want you for my bodyguard,'
the king told David, who replied:
'If I am fighting on your side,

you'll be amazed, I guarantee!'
(You will perceive the irony.)
Achish's leaders, when they heard,
dismissed the notion as absurd:
'He'll turn against us in the fight –
remember, he's an Israelite!'
There is no written proof at all
that David would have fought for Saul,
but Achish told him: 'It's no use –
my generals are so obtuse
we'd better cancel the idea.
They want your soldiers out of here!'
So David and his men departed*
before the bitter battle started –
rarely had Israel's pride sunk lower
than when they lost on Mount Gilboa!
Three princes fell, including Jon;
Saul knew his final hope had gone
when flights of arrows struck him too.
He told his servant: 'Run me through
before they get me!' 'No, my lord –
I'm frightened!' Saul took up his sword
and fell on it; and now we'll see
the start of David's monarchy...

* David discovered that Ziklag had been sacked in his absence. He recovered his wives, seized the raiders' plunder, and donated much of it to the tribe of Judah (see Chapter 8).

DAVID'S LAMENT FOR JONATHAN: 2 Samuel 1:19–27

With a grateful nod to Thomas Hardy: 'The Voice'.

Friend greatly loved, are you lost to me, lost to me?
Only the echo remains of your voice.
Slain at Gilboa, at such mortal cost to me!
Whisper in Ashkelon,* lest they rejoice.

* A Philistine city.

You who were all to me, never will call to me.
Prince of the King who made Philistines bleed!

Silent my harp-strings, which used to bind Saul to me.
Both of the mighty are fallen indeed!

Slain in the battle, you often appear to me
Twanging your bow as your enemies fell.
Love for a woman was never so dear to me;
Who shot the arrow that pierced me as well?

UNDER WHICH KING? 2 Samuel 2:1–3:5

Which side was David on? you'll ask.*
He knew he'd have a mammoth task
to gain the kingship after Saul –
he'd been an outlaw, after all!
He asked the Lord what he should do...
'Judah's the safest place for you,
since that's your tribe. Hebron is nice!'
So David took the Lord's advice,
decamped to Hebron, settled down,
and was awarded Judah's crown.
To have a *tribe* anoint a king
was not considered quite the thing –
it made the rest of them declare
for Ish-Bosheth, Saul's living heir.
So Joab, David's nephew, met*
the leader of Ish-Bosheth's set,
called Abner. From the troops they'd brought,

* Technically, after the disaster of Mount Gilboa, Israel was a defeated nation in thrall to the Philistines, from whom David had by now defected.

* Beside the Pool of Gideon.

these two selected twelve, who fought
for Israel's throne. The fighters grabbed
each other by the hair, and stabbed
but since each hit a vital spot,
it didn't really help a lot,
except to leave two dozen less.
Two kings, one people – what a mess!

PALACE INTRIGUES: 2 Samuel 3:1–4:12

Then King Ish-Bosheth heard a whisper
that Abner spent the night with Rizpah,
his father's concubine. 'Look here –
hands off the lady! Is that clear?'
Whether or not he'd shared her bed
(it's not confirmed), Abner saw red...
'I served your father faithfully,
but you'll get no more help from me!'
He went to Hebron, to support
King David's camp; but he was caught
by Joab, David's man as well,
who'd lost his brother Asahel
at Abner's hands. 'You are a spy!'
cried Joab (knowing it a lie),
'you're working for Ish-Bosheth's lot,
to see how much support we've got!'
He murdered Abner by the gate,
and David turned on him, irate.
'You shed this useful fellow's blood!
From this time on, your name is mud!'
But Joab was restored again
and made commander of his men...

CHAPTER 8

KING DAVID'S REIGN
(2 Samuel 4–24)

INTO DAVID'S CITY
(2 Samuel 4–6 & 1 Chronicles 11–15)

1. Short-cut to power (2 Samuel 4)

Though Ish-Bosheth stood in his way,
David was stricken with dismay
when he was brought the monarch's head
by Baanah and Recab,* who said:
'His father tried to murder you –
this was the least that we could do!'
True, Saul and he had not got on –
but David had been woebegone
when brought the news that he had died.*
So now, faced with this regicide
(although it sorted out the feud)
he didn't show much gratitude.
They dangled, minus hands and feet,
and he assumed Ish-Bosheth's seat...

* Two Benjamites.

* 2 Samuel 1:1–16.

2. Tunnelling (2 Samuel 5:6–12; 1 Chronicles 11:4–9)

Anointed as the Head of State,
King David thought he'd relocate
from distant Hebron, ruling them
from pivotal Jerusalem.*
The occupying Jebusites
called down from its commanding heights:
'You think you'll turn us out? You're kidding!'

* Jerusalem lay on the northern edge of Judah and the southern boundary of most of the other tribes' territories.

The walls were massive and forbidding,
but underneath there ran a shaft
to reach a spring, and David laughed.
'That's our way in, I think you'll find!'
The Jebusites were undermined...

3. Greeting the Ark (2 Samuel 6; 1 Chronicles 13 & 15)

The Ark was not esteemed by Saul
(it had been left, you will recall.
under Abinadab's protection).*
To set the seal on his election,
King David fetched the sacred chest,
and pitched a Tent,* where it would rest
till Solomon, his son, created
the Temple. As they celebrated
the Ark's arrival at the gate,
David got into quite a state,
leaping and dancing wildly
and showing off, for all to see,
his procreative apparatus.
'Why purposely humiliate us?'
Michal complained, 'showing your gear
to slave girls!' 'But the Lord was here,'
said David. 'In His sight, I tried
to seem low and undignified.
As for those slave girls – what they saw
should make them reverence me more!'
Michal withdrew from his embrace,
(they'd had no brood in any case).*

* 1 Sam 7:1.

* The Tabernacle.

* Although she had twice been David's wife, they do not appear to have had any children. She had five by her intermediate husband.

BATHSHEBA: 2 Samuel 11:1–12:25

1. The crime (11)

The day when Bathsheba decided to wash
caused a much bigger splash than she meant.
King David observed her proportions, said 'Gosh!',
and off to the palace she went...

He lay with her, and she conceived straight away,
so he sent for her husband Uriah.
'I've a letter for Joab* – deliver it, pray!'
The letter explained: 'I require...

* Besieging Rabbah, east of the Jordan.

'...Uriah (the bearer) to lead your attack.
When the enemy shoots from the wall,
make sure that the rest of your soldiers pull back –
he's the one I am anxious should fall!'

His commander obeyed, the manoeuvre was done,
and Uriah was killed, as agreed.
David married Bathsheba, who bore him a son;
but the Lord was displeased by the deed...

2. The parable of the ewe lamb (12:1–4)

The news that this decent man's life had been wrecked
caused Nathan the prophet unease...
He said to the king: 'Would you kindly reflect
on these words, and respond to them, please?

'A man of great wealth had a visitor come,
and he offered him something to eat.
It would hardly have cost a prohibitive sum
if his flocks had provided the meat...

'But the man had a neighbour; and all *he* possessed
was a ewe lamb he kept as a pet;
and when the rich fellow tucked in with his guest,
it was the man's pet that they ate!'

3. The reckoning (12:5–25)

King David (believing the story was true)
said to Nathan: 'That man ought to die
for being so mean!' 'But that person is *you*!
I'll explain, if you cannot see why...

'The Lord gave you riches upon your accession –
in fact, He'd have given you more.
And what did you do? Took Uriah's possession,
and killed him! You've flouted God's law...

'...so your son's life is forfeit; and one of these days
someone close to yourself will cavort
with your wives and bedfellows in full public gaze –
which can't be a very nice thought!'

'I deserve all I get!' murmured David, aghast.
'I am the most wretched of men!'
But thanks to Bathsheba, his gloom didn't last;
and soon she was pregnant again...*

* With Solomon.

DAVID v. ABSALOM: 2 Samuel 13:1–19:8

1. Family feud (13)

The son whom David loved the best
was Absalom,* who was distressed
when his blood-sister Tamar wailed:
'I fought to keep intact, and failed!'
Amnon,* the first of David's brood,

* His third son, by Maacah.

* Son of Ahinoam.

had forced her in a merry mood,
but Absalom retrieved her honour –
his eldest brother was a goner.
When David heard what had occurred,
conflicting loyalties were stirred –
he loved the killer, mourned the dead.
Meanwhile, Absalom had fled...

2. Winning votes (14:1–15:6)

The faithful Joab interceded.
It took some time,* but he succeeded,
and Absalom at last returned
(he'd had the crops of Joab burned
for not proceeding fast enough,
which strikes me as distinctly rough).
But David took too little care
to fetter Absalom... His hair
(which must have trailed along the floor)
scaled 2 kilograms or more
before he'd go to have it snipped –
all other men seemed nondescript
when matched against this flawless hunk.
Soon, any hopes of peace were sunk.
He'd stand before the city gate
and tell petitioners to wait
while he read through their brief. He'd say:
'King David can't see you today –
if *I* were judging in his place,
there's no doubt you would win your case!'
By seeming so accommodating
he steadily improved his rating...

* Three years before Absalom could return, and another two before David would see him.

3. Revolt (15:7–16:22)

After four years of self-promotion,
he thought he'd set the wheels in motion.

'Father, if it's all right with you
I'll go to Hebron.' 'What to do?'
'To thank the Lord for all He's done.'
Said David: 'Go in peace, my son!'
So off he went, and sent out word
that when the trumpet call was heard,
the tribes of Israel should shout:
'*King Absalom!*' 'Time to get out!'
said David, at this shattering news.
'He'll lay siege, and we're bound to lose.
Hurry – he'll soon be on his way!
Ten of my concubines can stay
to mind the shop.' Eastwards they fled,
taking the Ark; but then he said
(when they had crossed the Kidron Valley*):
'No – it must stay! Don't shilly-shally!
Return it to the Tabernacle.
If I can weather this débâcle
it will be waiting for me still –
if not, the Lord do what He will!'

* The valley separating Jerusalem and the Mount of Olives.

4. Fifth columnist (16:23–17:14)

The ladies David left behind
were well and truly concubined
by Absalom, in public view –
so Nathan's prophecy came true.*
King David's aide, Ahithophel
(hard to pronounce, harder to spell),
had joined up with the opposition,
becoming Absalom's tactician,
explaining that the obvious thing
was to pursue the fleeing king...
David had guessed what he would say,
and needed help to get away –
Hushai the Arkite was a friend
on whom he knew he could depend.

* When David returned, they were 'widowed', i.e., excluded from his household.

'Denounce Ahithophel,' he said,
'he's *got* to be discredited.
Make Absalom think you're the wiser,
rubbish the plan of his adviser,
and give us time to get a start!'
The faithful Hushai played his part...
'Long live the King, the Lord's Elect!'
'What made you suddenly defect?'
asked Absalom, suspiciously –
'you ought to love my Dad, not me!'
'I love the Throne, whose occupier
is you,' gushed the accomplished liar:
'The son is in the father's place!
Take my advice – do *not* give chase
(as prompted by Ahithophel)
until you have more personnel
to crush your father's lawless band.
Let them exceed the grains of sand
upon the shore – ride at their head!'
'I like it!' the usurper said...

5. Caught (17:15–18:18)

Ahithophel was quite disgusted
to learn he was no longer trusted,
and hanged himself. This daft delay
meant that King David got away,
making an unmolested flight
across the Jordan overnight
and ending up at Mahanaim,*
a place where friendly locals came
and brought them everything they lacked!
In due course, Absalom attacked...
They fought within a wood, which meant
a very nasty accident
unless they watched out for the trees.

* Where Jacob and his entourage camped before meeting Esau, after leaving Uncle Laban (Gen 32:1–2).

Despite his fighting expertise,
the king's son's challenge came to naught
when he was well and truly caught,
trapped in an oak branch by his hair
(his mule had left him dangling there).
The king had made his troops agree
to treat him like a VIP;
but Joab stabbed him to the heart,
and blew the trumpet to depart...

6. Grief (18:19–19:8)

King David had been told to wait
at Mahanaim, beside the gate,
instead of fighting with them too –
which was a prudent thing to do.
The watchman shouted out at last:
'Someone's approaching very fast,
and there's another following!'
The first to get there told the king:
'Good news! The Lord fought at this fight!'
'That's great – but is my boy all right?'
'I'm not quite sure,' the servant lied
(for he knew Absalom had died);
but then the second man arrived...
'Do you know if my son survived?'
the king asked. 'May his fate be shared
by all your foes!' the man declared –
and David guessed what this must mean.
Picture the lamentable scene!
'Oh Absalom, my son, my son!
If only I had been the one
who died today! Oh, woe is me!'
'This flood of tears lacks subtlety,'
said Joab (who was soon demoted*).
'Your troops were utterly devoted,

* 19:13.

and this is how you thank them! Great!
If you don't seem to celebrate,
they'll think you love your enemies
more than your friends!' These words of his
restored King David to his senses.
It was a time for mending fences...

CENSURED (2 Samuel 24, 1 Chronicles 21)

The Lord's wrath rose against His race,*
and so, to put them in their place,
He worked upon the hapless king
and made him do a sinful thing,
which made his subjects pay the price...
David thought: 'Wouldn't it be nice
to have my total forces counted?'
And so he did. Their strength amounted
to well over a million men;
but Joab (here he is again!)
explained that numbers didn't count –
God would provide the right amount
to win his battles when he must;
his census thus implied mistrust.*
To pay for his impiety,
God told him: 'Choose from 1–3...
(1) Three years' famine and starvation;
(2) Three months' utter subjugation;
or (3) a plague – it's up to you.'
'Oh, 1 or 3 – don't send us 2!'
The Lord chose 3, which swept the land,
but the avenging Angel's hand
drew back (to everybody's wonder)
before Jerusalem went under.
God had sublimed His irritation;
the sudden wave of devastation

* In 1 Chr 21:1 it is stated that 'Satan rose up against Israel' and prompted David's census. This is the first time I have noticed a reference to the Devil in the history of the Hebrews.

* Theologians still discuss the 'sinfulness' of David's census: this is one suggestion.

left 70,000 people dead.
'All right – call it a day!' He said,
'that is the number I require!'
The plague had got to Mount Moriah*
where Araunah, a Jebusite,
was farming on its fertile height.
'I want to buy some land from you –
your splendid threshing-floor would do,'
the king explained, 'and there I'll build
an altar, before more are killed.*
Tell me the price you have in mind!'
'The land is yours – in fact, I'll find
some oxen, plus what you require
to build a sacrificial fire.
I've loads of wood, as you can see!'
'My sacrifice must not be free,'
David replied, 'so I shall pay;
but thank you kindly anyway!'
And so the king assuaged his guilt –
and here the Temple would be built...

* This hill, which became the Temple Mount, is also traditionally associated with Abraham's near-sacrifice of Isaac (Gen 22).

* David is unaware that the Lord has already decided to call off the pestilence.

CHAPTER 9

NOT WISE ENOUGH... (1 Kings 1–12; 1 Chronicles 28–2 Chronicles 9)

FAMILY FEUD (again): 1 Kings 1–2

King David started to decline...
They warmed him with a concubine,
but when he failed to possess her,
the gossip turned to his successor.
Adonijah said: 'I'm the one!'
(he was the oldest living son)*
and Joab backed him. David, though,
said to Bathsheba: 'As you know,
I promised you that when I'm gone
the throne should go to Solomon –
your son and mine. You have my word!'
With great display he was interred,
and Solomon was crowned. He slew
Adonijah, and Joab too,
as well as other malcontents.
So let the Golden Age commence!

* There was a second son, Kileab, but he is never mentioned again (2 Sam 3:3).

CRASH COURSE: 1 Kings 3:4–15, 2 Chronicles 1:7–12

The Lord found Solomon in bed,
and as the monarch dreamed, He said:
'I'll give you what you most desire.'
'Well, what I'm going to require
to govern this enormous nation
are lessons in administration!'
The Lord agreed: 'No legislator
will be your equal, now or later.
Wisdom and Justice* will be yours
(as long as you respect my laws);
and since you didn't ask for gold
your riches will be manifold!'

* Summarized at 1Kgs 4:29–34.

SWORD OF JUSTICE: 1 Kings 3:16–28

The only case we see him judge
concerns two women with a grudge,
and neither of the two would budge
till they had said their bit.

The plaintiff, an impassioned mother,
sought retribution from the other.
'She managed, while she slept, to smother
her baby, squashing it...

'...and then sneaked up to me in bed,
gave me the infant that was dead,
and called *my* baby *hers* instead –
a crime you can't permit!'

'That's rubbish!' the defendant cried.
'It was *her* infant that had died –
she wants to grab *mine* out of pride,
and that's an end of it!'

'I see,' said Solomon the Wise.
'One story is a pack of lies
and one's the truth... What I'd advise
is that the baby's split...

'...between the two of you!' 'No, lord!'
the plaintiff cried, seeing the sword:
'Although that woman is a fraud,
let her keep all of it!'

The other said: 'Cut it in two!
That's much the wisest thing to do –
he won't belong to me or you!'*
'That's quite true, I admit...'

* Although this response is dramatically necessary, it seems odd that the baby-snatcher doesn't agree with the plaintiff and keep the whole baby.

...said Solomon, 'which proves to me
that you're not very motherly.
The plaintiff spoke more tenderly,
and therefore, I submit...

'...*she is the mother*! Next case, please!'
Dumbfounded by his expertise,
the Israelites fell on their knees –
the new king was a hit!

BUILDING OPERATIONS: 1 Kings 5–9 (2 Chronicles 2–7)

The Temple-building operation
(with detailed specification

and notes upon the different stages)
goes on for literally pages.
The cedar that they would require
was grown by Hiram, King of Tyre
(the capital of Lebanon)
where 30,000 slaves had gone
to get the forest giants falling.
To do the necessary hauling
demanded 70,000 more –
plus 80,000 men to saw
and shape the stone exactly right.*
No hammers could be used onsite,
since *quietness* was stipulated:
so it was all prefabricated
to guarantee a perfect fit,
just like a self-assembly kit.
It took them seven years to make;
once this was done, they had to take
100,000 sheep and goats
(plus oxen too), and slit their throats...
Now that the Ark was safe and sound,
the king built, on adjacent ground,
his palace, with its cedar cladding.
He finished off the job by adding
the queen's pad (also lined with cedar),
where he could go if he should need her.

* The Temple's dimensions were no greater than those of an English parish church, so it is hard to understand why a workforce of almost 200,000 was needed.

TRADE SURPLUS

His kingdom, at its height, extended
beyond where Moses had intended –
from the Euphrates in the east
to Egypt!* Petty wars had ceased,
and, safe from imminent attacks,

* 1 Kgs 4:20–25.

the population could relax
beneath their fig tree and their vine.
Its economic growth was fine...
The splendid chariots they made*
bolstered a buoyant export trade† –
25 tons of gold per year
made lesser problems disappear
(and don't forget the revenue
his tax collectors brought in too!).‡
The Queen of Sheba's famous trip§
to quiz him on his scholarship
by asking what are called 'hard questions'
has naturally raised suggestions
about the vibes between the pair,
which I suspect are all hot air;
more rational opinion thinks
they were discussing trading links...

* 1Kgs 10:29/2 Chr 1:17.

† Solomon's fabled copper mines were supposed to be a good money-earner, but there is no mention of them in the Bible.

‡ 10:14–15/2 Chr 9:13–14.

§ 10:1–13/2 Chr 9:1–12.

SOLOMON'S BLUNDER: 1 Kings 11

Then everything went pear-shaped. Why?
Well, for a start, he didn't try
to regulate his sexual urge.
From the statistics that emerge
(and even if they've been inflated)
this monarch must have generated
an excess of testosterone.
Three hundred concubines alone
would stretch most males, I'd have thought;
and Solomon's majestic court
included *700* wives!
No inventory, alas, survives
of who they were, or whom they bore,
perhaps because he broke the law

in marrying outside his race,
exacerbating his disgrace
by worshipping their gods instead.
The Lord, as you'd expect, saw red...
'You've turned from me, so I've decided
to have your kingdom sub-divided.
I'll leave all the Judean lands
in your son Rehoboam's hands
(he'll keep King David's City too);
but ten tribes* I will snatch from you,
and they'll select another king –
King Jeroboam!' Panicking,
King Solomon arranged a hit,
but Jeroboam heard of it
and fled to Egypt, where he hid
till it was time to make his bid...

* The tribe of Benjamin allied itself with its neighbour Judah (12:21).

THE SPLIT: 1 Kings 12:1–20 (2 Chronicles 10)

King Solomon declined and died...
The people met his heir, and cried:
'Your father's yoke has weighed us down –
improve things, and you'll get the crown!'
The Lord made Rehoboam say
(to get the break-up under way):
'*Improve* your lot? The life you led
will feel like a feather bed
compared with what I'm going to do!
You felt his whip – I'll flail you
with scorpions!' As you'd expect,
this had a negative effect...
Ten of the tribes said: 'On your bike!
We'll find another king we like,
and let the House of David rot!'

But those of Judah's tribe did not,
nor did the house of Benjamin –
and so the dual reigns begin.
King Jeroboam was selected
to rule the tribes that had defected,
now known as *Israel*. Henceforth
one realm is South, and one is North.*

* Israel is often referred to as the Northern Kingdom.

EXCITING TIMES AHEAD...

Thirty-nine monarchs will be crowned
before the end of Kings Book 2;
more bad than good ones will be found,
and many vanish in a coup...

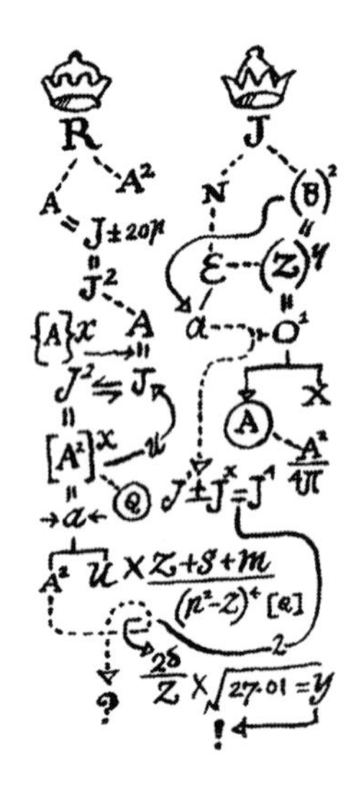

...till foreign powers overthrow
both nations, as you'll shortly see.
Israel is the first to go
(in 722 BC)...

...when the Assyrians invade
and sweep them off. Judah fights on
till 586, when they are made
to sit and weep in Babylon!

Some kings stand out (though most do not);
two prophets are a major hit!*
Since I can't versify the lot,
let's look at a notorious bit...

* Elijah and Elisha.

CHAPTER 10

THE DIVIDED KINGDOM (1 Kings 12–2 Kings 25)*

THE MONARCHS OF JUDAH AND ISRAEL

Scripture gives the beginning of each monarch's reign with reference to the year of the opposing monarch's reign. I have used this information to show which were reigning simultaneously. A tick or cross indicates their merit in the eyes of the Lord, as judged by the scribe.

* 2 Chr describes the history of Judah, but not of Israel (Chapters 11–36).

I = inherited crown, U = usurped crown.

JUDAH	ISRAEL
×Rehoboam (I)	×Jeroboam I (U)
×Abijah (I)	
✓Asa (I)	
	×Nadab (I)
	×Baasha (U)
	×Elah (I)
	×Zimri (U)
	×Omri (U)
	×Ahab (I)
✓Jehoshaphat (I)	
	×Ahaziah (I)
	×Joram or Jehoram (I)
×Joram or Jehoram (I)	
×Azahiah (I)	
×Athaliah (U)*	
	✓Jehu (U)

The Age of Jezebel, wife of King Ahab

* Ahaziah's violent mother; the only queen to rule. If baby Joash had not been hidden, she would have ended David's direct line (2 Kgs 11:1–3).

✓Joash or Jehoash (I)	
	×Jehoahaz or Joahaz (I)
	×Joash or Jehoash (I)
✓Amaziah (I)	
	×Jeroboam II (I)
✓Uzziah or Azariah (I)	
	×Zechariah (I)
	×Shallum (U)
	×Menahem (U)
	×Pekaniah (I)
	×Pekah (U)
✓Jotham (I)	
×Ahaz (I)	
	×Hoshea (U) *Israel overthrown 722*BC
✓Hezekiah (I)	
×Manasseh (I)	
×Amon (I)	
✓Josiah (I)	
×Jehoahaz or Joahaz (I)	
×Jehoiakim (I)	
×Jehoiachin (I) *Deported with some of the population*	
×Zedekiah or Mattaniah (I) *Judah overthrown* 586BC	

THE CONTEXT...

To start with, both the nations warred –

Judah was favoured by the Lord
because He'd had a tender spot
for David (though he'd sinned a lot).
But after years of to-and-fro
they settled for the status quo,
since Israel's unstable throne
was rocked by crises of its own.
Usurpers number half their kings –
hardly a happy state of things!
By contrast, Judah's monarchy
kept David's line intact – the key
to Joseph's later royal link
(at least, so Luke and Matthew think).
But, talking of these kings, it's odd
how many turned away from God!
Each monarch gets an entry, stating
his Scriptural approval rating –
the tick or cross I have appended
shows if they pleased Him, or offended.
King Ahab was among the worst.
His reign was fated from the first,

through marrying a Wife from Hell –
the celebrated Jezebel...

THE AGE OF JEZEBEL: 1 Kings 16:29–2 Kings 9:37

1. Enter Elijah (1 Kings 16:29–17:6)

Ahab was Israel's seventh king.*
He irked the Lord like anything
by setting up a shrine to Baal;
and so God made the harvest fail,
and sent Elijah to explain:
'The Lord's put *me* in charge of rain!'
(Elijah's standing is immense
in both the Bible's Testaments;
when Jesus Christ was crucified,
some thought it was to him he cried.)*
The prophet instantly departed,
since Jezebel, by now, had started
enforcing zero toleration
on people of his faith and station.
The Lord told him to hide away.
'Ravens will call by twice a day
to bring you rations, till you hear
it's safe for you to reappear!'

* He was the son of King Omri, who, interestingly, is the first Old Testament figure to be mentioned in a non-Biblical contemporary record. His name is found on the Stela of King Mesha of Moab, *c.*830 BC.

* Matt 27:47 and Mark 15:35.

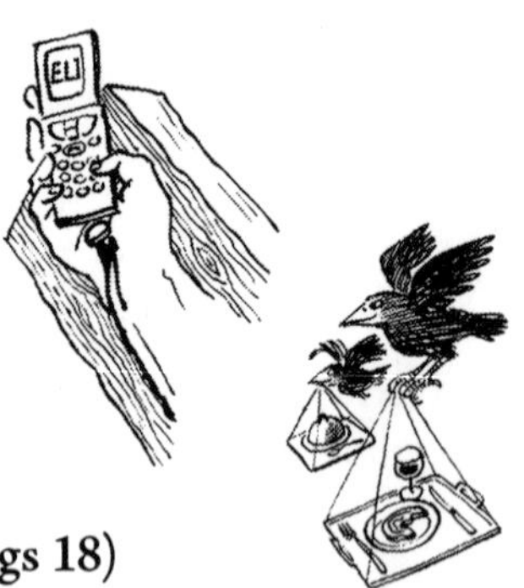

2. The showdown with Baal (1 Kings 18)

King Ahab's base, Samaria,*
was a disaster area.
Three rainless seasons had gone by
without a cloud to stain the sky,
so God despatched the Weather Tsar
to meet the king. 'Oh, there you are!'
cried Ahab. 'Can't you end this drought?'

* The kings of Israel had adopted Samaria as their capital, in opposition to Jerusalem.

Elijah said: 'It's come about
because you have ignored the Lord –
a gesture you can ill-afford,
for He is greater than the rest.
Why don't we put it to the test?
Bring all the prophets you require,
and see if they can start a fire
by using pure Baal-force
(no matches are allowed, of course).
Then *I'll* try, with the Lord's support.'
Vast crowds arrived to watch the sport –
almost a thousand prophets came
to light a flame in Baal's name,
but though they danced till nearly dark,
they couldn't even raise a spark,
so faith in Baal started dwindling!
Elijah then arranged his kindling,
and raised the odds by drenching it
till no one could have got it lit...
'Oh Lord, reform your people's ways
by sending us a proper blaze!'
the prophet cried. Wow, what a sight!
The earth and boulders caught alight,
and all the Israelites applauded...
Elijah had the prophets sworded,
and said to Ahab: 'Hitch your horses –
the roads will soon be water-courses!'
The clouds came up, the heavens burst;
he ran ahead,* and got home first.

* 'Tucking his cloak into his belt' – a vivid touch (1 Kgs 18:46).

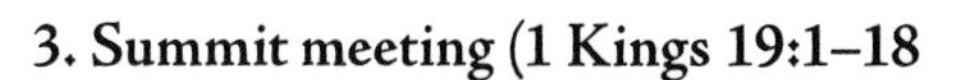

3. Summit meeting (1 Kings 19:1–18

Elijah then received a note
from Jezebel, in which she wrote:
The gods' revenge fall on my head
if, by tomorrow, you're not dead!

It took him forty days and nights
to reach Mount Sinai, on whose heights
Moses alone had ever stepped.*
He climbed it, found a cave, and slept
until the Lord asked: 'What's up?' 'Well,
the energetic Jezebel
has slaughtered everyone but me
who's got some skill in prophecy!'
'I see... Just step outside, will you?
I'll very soon be passing through!'
Rocks split before Elijah's eyes,
but God did not materialize
within the storm; nor did He stride
across the quaking mountainside;
nor was He in the flame and smoke
that followed. When at last He spoke,
He sounded faint, as if subdued;*
however, this belied His mood.
'Obey these orders faithfully...
The Israelites that turned from me
must die (not more than 7K
proved truly steadfast, by the way).
Firstly, anoint the Syrian king
Hazael,* and let him have his fling –
he's bound to massacre a few!'
He then gave Order No. 2:
'Make sure that Jehu* gets the crown;
he'll cut the Baal-servers down
that dodge Hazael's busy blade.
And (3) – I want arrangements made
to have Elisha take your seat –
the cleaning-up will be complete
once he has axed the final few.
Those are the thing's you've got to do!'

* And possibly Joshua.

* A still, small voice.

* King of the Arameans, the Biblical name for Syria.

* The one king of Israel with a positive credit rating.

Elijah did the tasks God set,
though Ahab ruled for some time yet;
the great mistake that cost his throne
was going in for grow-your-own...

4. Naboth's vineyard (1 Kings 21)

A vineyard, Naboth's property,
had long been in his family.
Ahab (who wanted to be able
to pick fresh produce for his table)
told him: 'Your plot is near my gate –
I'd like us to negotiate...
I'll either pay the market price
or find you somewhere just as nice!'
Naboth replied: 'The Lord forbid!
I've farmed it as my fathers did –
I'm simply not prepared to sell!'
The angry king told Jezebel,
who paid two scoundrels to proclaim
that Naboth had abused the name
of God and king. So he was stoned,
and Ahab seized the plot he'd owned...

God called Elijah. 'Tell the king:
"The Lord dislikes this sort of thing.
The dogs lapped up the blood you spilled
when you had guiltless Naboth killed –
they'll drink yours also, when you lie
where he lay when condemned to die –
and later on, they'll eat your wife!"'
The king then led a better life,
so God decided to delay
the onset of the fateful day...

5. Elisha, miracle-worker (2 Kings 2 and 4)

Elijah knew his time was near,

and primed Elisha for his place.
'If you *observe* me disappear
you will inherit twice my grace!'

A chariot of fire came by –
he vanished in a cloud of smoke.
Elisha, with a mournful cry,
picked up his master's fallen cloak...

Long, long before (during the Flight),
God intervened on quite a scale:
supplies of manna every night;*
the Red Sea split;† thousands of quail‡...

* Ex 16:14.
† Ex 14:21.
‡ Ex 16:13.

But people during Ahab's reign
received more *personal* attention –
a widow's dead son lived again,
thanks to Elijah's intervention*...

* 1 Kgs 17:7–24.

...and now Elisha, too, was keen
to help with problems of this type.
Two instances show what I mean –
assistance without lots of hype!

*Oil supplies (4:1–7)**
A widow was in debt. 'I've got
a little oil in a cup!'
'Assemble every empty pot
that you can find, and fill them up...'

* The miracle of the widow's cruse.

Feeding the hundred (4:42–44)
A man had twenty loaves of bread...
'I've got a hundred here to feed!'
'And so you will,' Elisha said,
'God's bakery will meet their need!'

6. Micaiah ignored... (1 Kings 22)

King Ahab had arranged a chat
with Judah's king, Jehoshaphat
(who gets a tick). 'It makes me mad
to think that Ramoth-Gilead
was seized from us by Aram's king,*
and we're not doing anything!'
Jehoshaphat said: 'Need a hand?
We are one people and one land;
my horses gallop with your horses;
we'll fight with our combined resources –
but first let's hear some prophesying!'
King Ahab's prophets started lying
about a comprehensive win;
Jehoshaphat, not taken in,
asked for a seer of the Lord
to see if He was in accord.
'There's one here somewhere, called Micaiah,'
Ahab replied, 'but he's a liar –
he always forecasts gloom and doom!'
Micaiah came into the room
predicting outright victory.
Ahab was thrown. 'Don't lie to me!
Now tell the truth!' 'All right – I lied,'
the prophet openly replied:
'These optimistic prophecies
come from the Lord – a ploy of His
to make you gallop to your fate.
In truth, disaster lies in wait!'

* Ben-Hadad. Hazael had not yet succeeded to the Aramean throne.

'Oh yes?' sneered Ahab, 'what's the betting?
A low-fat diet's all you're getting*
till I return victorious!'
His ending was inglorious:
he fought the battle in disguise
to hide his crown from foreign eyes,
but someone scored a random hit
(though God may well have helped a bit).

* Bread and water.

7. Going to the dogs (2 Kings 9)

Two sons of Ahab, in succession,
kept Israel's throne in their possession,
and Judah rallied to their cause
in various external wars.
The King of Judah, Ahaziah,
went to Jezreel, to enquire
about King Joram (Ahab's second)*
who wasn't well. Elisha reckoned
that if he sorted out these two
he would achieve a major coup.
He told a prophet from his team:
'The time is ripe, the need extreme!
Fly swiftly as the wind, and see
Commander Jehu secretly.
Anoint him Israel's king – then run!'
After the blessing had been done,
the new King Jehu rode like mad
with all the cavalry he had
towards Jezreel, where he shot
King Joram on poor Naboth's plot,
piercing the fellow through the heart.
(The King of Judah had a start,
but he was caught, and died as well.)
The noise attracted Jezebel;
to give herself the moral edge

* His older brother, Ahab's successor, died after falling through a window (2 Kgs 1). This is called *defenestration*.

she leaned over her window ledge,
located on an upper floor,
revealing much, or maybe more
(her eyes made up, her hair just so),
saw Joram's slaughterer below,
and gave a diabolic shriek:
'Usurper Zimri reigned a week – *
that's all *you'll* do!' But she descended
a little quicker than intended,
when, at King Jehu's urgent shout,
the lady's eunuchs threw her out.
Below the wall that skirts Jezreel,
the dogs enjoyed a proper meal
(her head, though, was too hard to eat;
nor would they touch her hands and feet.)

* The fifth king of Israel (1 Kgs 16:15–20).

That was the end of the Age of Jezebel

ISRAEL FALLS: 2 Kings 15:17–17:41

Assyria expanded west...
King Menahem* had thought it best
to pay 1,000 silver talents
to keep them off – this shaky balance
survived until King Pekah's reign,*
who gave up part of his domain;
the residents were relocated,
the hapless king was liquidated,
and Hoshea,* an appointee,
ruled what was left. His treachery
(he'd asked for help from Egypt's king)
completely ruined everything,
and Israel was at last dismembered.
The only way it was remembered

* *c.*745–738.

* *c.*737–732.

* *c.*732–724.

In 722.

was through the people later called
Samaritans. Jews were appalled
at this degraded, hybrid race,
which they considered a disgrace
for marrying outside their kind –
not what the Lord God had in mind!*
Now Judah had to face the fact
that it was bound to be attacked...

* This is why the Good Samaritan in Jesus's parable is so remarkable (Luke 10:30).

JUDAH FINDS A PROPHET...: 2 Kings 16–19

King Ahaz* had been threatened too,
and shared the Northern Kingdom's view
that peace was better bought than won.
So gold and silver by the ton,

* *c.*735–715.

stripped from the Temple of the Lord
(together with the massive hoard
the kings of Judah owned as well)
bought time. But after Israel fell,
Judah's new monarch, Hezekiah,
began to *fight* the occupier!
Sennacherib, Assyria's king,
told him: 'You can't do anything
against our might, so sign a truce –
your Lord is not the slightest use!'
Isaiah (yes, the very same

c. 715–687.

whose writings, some believe, proclaim
the birth of Jesus*) was offended...
'Jerusalem will be defended
against this devotee of Baal –
his siege is guaranteed to fail!'
God killed the soldiers in their tents*
before they mounted their offence;
Sennacherib stopped the attack,
left Judah, and did not come back...

* Was Hezekiah the 'saviour' promised in Isaiah's famous passage about a young woman giving birth to a child, which is so often quoted at Christmas (Isaiah 7:14)?

* 185,000 of them.

...OF DOOM!: 2 Kings 20:12–25:21

Some strangers came from Babylon
to meet the king. When they had gone
Isaiah asked: 'what did they see?'
'Everything that belongs to me –
and that's a lot!' said Hezekiah,
'so they had plenty to admire!'
The prophet told him: 'They'll be back
(this time with a capacious sack)
and drag off your descendants, too –
so says the Lord!' His words came true...
As Babylon increased in strength,
Assyria declined; at length
the kings of Judah were in thrall
to Babylon. The last of all
was Zedekiah, puppet king,*
who did a very silly thing
and fought against his foreign master,
which only made the end come faster.
It was a war he couldn't win,
and so Jerusalem caved in
to King Nebuchadnezzar's force.
They put it to the torch, of course,

* *c.*597–587.

In 586.

and Judah's upper class were sent
to Babylon and banishment.*
Beside its waters, in despair
(with hanging baskets everywhere)
they sat and wept, their harps unplayed,*
regretting the mistakes they'd made.

* The Babylonians left the agricultural workforce, to keep the economy going.

* Psalm 137.

CHAPTER 11

AFTER THE FALL... (Ezra–Jonah)

The second half of the Old Testament (after 2 Chronicles) consists of twenty-four books, varying in length from very long (Isaiah, sixty-six chapters) to very short (Obadiah, twenty-one verses). Two books are written in verse or melodic form – Psalms and The Song of Solomon.

Some describe the return to Jerusalem and its surrounding lands after the fifty-year exile, the rebuilding of the Temple (finished in 515 BC), and the redistribution of territories. The Books of Ezra, Nehemiah, Esther and Daniel all have a substantial historical content.

The most numerous books are 'prophetic' – visionary or contemplative works inspired by God's punishment for His people's sins (by letting Jerusalem fall), and hopes of a new start. Isaiah is the most famous of these.

Finally, there are some 'oddities'. The Books of Job and Jonah are the stories of men made into agents of God's will. The Book of Ecclesiastes is a downbeat reflective work ('all is in vain') that seems to owe nothing to any other Old Testament writing.

1. FOUR 'HISTORICAL' BOOKS

The Books of Ezra and Nehemiah

Nebuchadnezzar's royal line
would last for only fifty years.
With Babylon in steep decline
another conqueror appears...

Meet Cyrus! He's the Persian king
Took Babylon 539 BC.
who said to Judah's folk: 'Return!'
The process of resettling
is found in Ezra. Here you'll learn...

...about the Temple's restoration,
Completed 515.
and how the outcasts of the race
(Israel's scattered population)
worked hard to stop this taking place.
Ezra 4:1–5:12.

Then priestly Ezra and his crew
checked Judah's racial purity,
deporting wives (and children too)
whose genes were not what they should be!
9–10.

You'll find in Nehemiah's* book
* Governor of Judah *c*.440.
how they rebuilt the city wall.
Fifty-two days was all it took,
with God to mastermind it all.
Neh 6:1–16.

Then Nehemiah reinstated
observance of the Sabbath day.
13:15–22.
And, just like Ezra, stipulated
that foreign wives be sent away...
13:23–30.

The Book of Esther

The Persian queen* was in disgrace...
She had been ordered to appear
and share the royal feast. 'No fear!'
she told King Xerxes,† 'I'll keep clear
till you have sobered up, my dear!'
Which meant a vacant place...

* Queen Vashti.

† c.485–465.

A Jew named Mordecai lived there,
and brought his lovely ward (named Esther)
before the monarch. He assessed her,
invited her to his siesta,
and after he'd undressed/possessed her,
he queened her, unaware...

...that she was *Jewish*! Stiff with pride,
Mordecai did not genuflect
to Haman (of the King's Elect),
who told the king: 'This scornful sect
show absolutely no respect –
I've planned their genocide!'

Queen Esther cooked a meal for three –
Haman, the king, and lots of booze...
The king said: 'Esther, you can choose
your dearest wish!' 'Then save the Jews –

for I'm one too. You *must* refuse
to back his policy!'

Exit the king, distressed for Esther,
and Haman falls upon his knees
beside the queen. 'Forgive me, please!
I'll reinstate you deportees!'
Enter the king: 'How dare you squeeze
the queen, you base molester!'

The wretch was now as good as dead...
He'd built a gallows very high*
on which to dangle Mordecai;
but now his plans had gone awry,
he was the culprit they would tie
the noose-rope to instead!

* About 23 metres.

PS. His ten sons also died
before the queen was mollified...

The Book of Daniel (1:3-16)

1. Food Freak (1:3–16)

In Babylon, they liked to train
the brightest Jews for some vocation.
Since Daniel had a first-class brain,
he started studying *translation*.

They ate well on this training scheme –
but he and his three friends pursued
a vegetarian regime,
and just drank water with their food.

The steward told them: 'If the king
observes your undernourishment,
compared with all the rest, I'll swing!'
'We'll set up an experiment...'

the bright lad said. 'We four maintain
our veggie diet to the letter;
then match us with the rest again,
and see if *they* or *we* look better!'*

* A very early example of the scientific method.

The steward couldn't understand –
they'd won by eating *vegetation*!
So saturated fats were banned,
and pulses were the new sensation...

2. The fiery furnace (3:1-30)

Nebuchadnezzar was the king.
He had an idol made of gold
that people started worshipping.
But three refused, so we are told.

This hurt Nebuchadnezzar's ego
(my desperate attempt to rhyme
Shadrach, Meshach and Abednego,
the perpetrators of this crime).

'You'll singe for scorning me!' he cried,
so in the furnace they were thrown,
but simply walked around inside,
unharmed. Nor were the three alone...

A godlike *fourth* could be detected.
The king shrieked: 'Come out right away!
Of course your god must be respected –
I'll raise your rank and up your pay!'

3. The writing on the wall (5:1-31)

Nebuchadnezzar's son now reigned,
and he, Belshazzar, had a feast
when countless guests were entertained.
The merriment abruptly ceased...

...when he beheld a frightening sight –
a hand that wrote upon the wall.
It put him off his food all right!
His wise men hurried to his call...

...and read the words, but couldn't tell
what MENE, MENE, TEKEL meant;
nor did UPHARSIN ring a bell.
His queen advised: 'Have Daniel sent...

'...he's good at solving things like this.'
So Daniel came. 'A piece of cake!
The words proclaim your nemesis.
Your father was prepared to make...

'...obeisance to the One True Lord,
but you've been rather less devout,
so you will earn your just reward.
I'll show you how I've worked that out...

'MENE – you've almost run your course.
TEKEL – you've not come up to scratch.
UPHARSIN means the Persian force
is coming – and you'll lose the match.'

Despite this downbeat prophecy,
he was bequeathed a golden chain
and raised in rank to No. 3.
That very night, the king was slain...

4. Thrown to the lions (6:1-24)

King Darius ruled Babylon
(the Persian leader, as you've guessed),
and he and Daniel got on,
to the annoyance of the rest.

They came up with a bright idea,
and told the king: 'Sign a decree
that makes it absolutely clear –
No one shall pray except to me!'

An edict Daniel ignored –
three times a day he'd kneel and face
Jerusalem, and greet the Lord.
'You can't make him a special case,' ...

...the king was told by Daniel's foes,
gleeful to see what he was doing.
'Into the lions' den he goes –
Bon appetit, and happy chewing!'

The king arrived before the sun,
discovered him alive and well,
and fed the beasts with everyone
who'd had it in for Daniel.

2. ISAIAH, A 'PROPHETIC' BOOK

I have selected three chapters from Isaiah, which are often supposed to anticipate the coming of a 'Messiah', who will unify and exalt the Jewish nation.

Isaiah Chapter 7: God with us

Isaiah told Ahaz,* King of Judah:
'You're going to face a worse intruder
than Israel or Aramea –
Assyria will soon be here!
Those nations will be torn in two;
if you don't keep faith, so will you!'
God tried to make him less depressed:
'I'll send a sign, upon request –
say when and where.' But Ahaz said:
'I must not test God, so I've read.'*
Isaiah snapped. 'You've got a cheek!
That's *not* the way you ought to speak
to God the Father, all-divine!
Now listen – this will be the sign
(I asked Him, which *you* should have done!)...
The woman will produce a son – *
Emmanuel will be his name,
which means *God with us*. All the same,
before the lad knows left from right,
Assyria's aggressive might
will crush those enemies you faced –
and Judah too will be laid waste,
its fields choked with briar and thorn –
no vines, no pasture, and no corn.
Honey and curds will be your fare.
But God's still with you – don't despair!'

* *c.*735–715.

* e.g. Deut 6:16.

*'Look – the young woman is now with child' may be the best translation. This is often quoted as a prediction of the coming of Jesus, but it more probably refers to King Ahaz's queen, who gave birth to Hezekiah, the hoped-for deliverer of Judah.

Isaiah Chapter 9: Light in the Darkness

When the Twelve Tribes are mentioned, a few get ignored,
like Naphtali and Zebulun, scorned by the Lord
(perhaps they were almost forgotten by Him,
up in Gentile Galilee, out on a limb).
But later He honoured them both, and a light
has now dawned upon those who were living in night!*
How happy He made them – like mountains of grain
freshly threshed, or the plunder from those they had slain!
He has broken their yoke beyond risk of renewal;
their enemies' war-gear makes excellent fuel;
and we're blessed with a Child, our son, whom we call
our Wonderful Counsellor, God over All,
our Father Eternal, our Patron of Peace!
The sway of his sceptre will ever increase
as he sits on King David's illustrious throne,
and rules us by Justice and Wisdom alone.
The Lord God Almighty will make this come true.
[Isaiah, once more, takes a positive view.]

* This reading is favoured by the Authorized Version and some modern texts. A different 'take' is read at Christmas, when it seems to *foretell* a universal 'coming of the light', rather than referring to it as a provincial episode, as here.

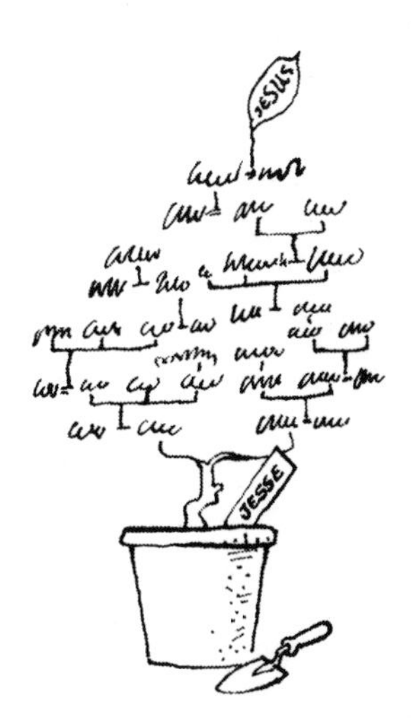

Isaiah Chapter 11: Jesse's Tree revitalized

From the stump of Jesse's Tree
(David's genealogy)
comes renewed vitality.
What a branch it's raising!

See what Fruit the branch will bear!
He'll spread Justice everywhere...
Of the Spirit, all will share,
with God Himself liaising!

Eyes and ears can mislead...
Essential facts are all he'll need
when he arrives to intercede,
with righteousness appraising...

Harmony will be complete...
Wolf and lion go off meat...
Lamb's no longer good to eat...
Side by side they're grazing...

He'll reclaim his scattered nation,
ending eastern domination.
Back they come in jubilation
down the trail He's blazing!

Moab, Edom and the rest
sprung on, slaughtered and suppressed...
Judah will have come off best –
won't that be amazing?

3. THREE CURIOUS BOOKS

The Book of Job

The Devil told the Lord one day:
'I've combed the earthly globe
for someone good in every way.'
The Lord replied: 'Meet Job!

'He keeps my Law in everything –
there's righteousness for you!'

'I'm not surprised, considering
the man's so well-to-do!

'But wreck his household and denude
his flocks, and then you'll see
a rather different attitude –
that I can guarantee!'

'All right,' said God, 'we'll have a test...
Upset his peace of mind
until he's utterly depressed –
then see how he's inclined!'

Disaster struck out of the blue...
Job's sons and daughters dead...
His flocks gone, and his camels too...
He wept, and shaved his head.

'Naked I first breathed God's sweet air,
and naked I will die.
He gives and takes our destined share –
all praise to Him on High!'

Three friends* exclaimed: 'You're in this plight
because you disobeyed.
You've earned your punishment, all right!'
Job, utterly dismayed...

* 'Job's comforters'.

...replied: 'But I am not to blame!
What have I done or said?'
His wife agreed: 'Go, curse God's name –
dare Him to strike you dead!'

Our hero wished he *could* have died,
but God he would not curse...

'If it's His will, I must abide,
for better or for worse!'

Job's perseverance pleased the Lord,
for He had won His bet!
He had his servant's flocks restored,
and made him richer yet...

The Book of Jonah

The Lord told Jonah: 'Work to do!
The Ninevites* are so debased
I shouldn't think you've ever faced
their equal. There's no time to waste!
Save them – now off with you!'

* Inhabitants of Nineveh, the Assyrian capital.

But Jonah went the other way,
refusing to obey the Lord.
He found a boat he could afford,
said 'Tarshish* – single,' went aboard,
and in the hold he lay...

* Possibly a drunken form of Tarsus in modern Turkey.

A storm broke; they began to sink.
'You've caused this wind!' the sailors cried,
'how can your God be pacified?'
'Just pick me up,' Jonah replied,
'and drop me in the drink!'

The crew reluctantly obeyed.
But Jonah was not meant to die...
A great fish* that was swimming by
consumed him. Feeling warm and dry,
our grateful hero prayed...

* Not a whale, at least according to the Bible.

'Lord, thanks for sending me this fish –
it's more help than I thought I'd get!
That was my hairiest moment yet!
Bring me to land, for I'm all set
to carry out your wish!'

So off to Nineveh he goes...
'Your wicked ways are widely known!
This city will be overthrown
unless you rapidly atone!'
The outcome, as the sequel shows...

...explains his earlier behaviour.
The city instantly repents,
so the compassionate Lord relents –
but Jonah bitterly resents
being the people's saviour!

He tells the Lord: 'Can't you see why
I acted in that furtive fashion?
These people don't deserve compassion!
I really think you ought to ration
your love and grace – please try!'

The book's last lines show God defending
His policy of lending grace
to those not of His chosen race.*
Jonah's put firmly in his place –
but it's a curious ending...

* Evangelizing non-Hebrews is certainly not a feature of the Old Testament. Does the fable have its origins in the Samaritan community of mixed races?

The Book of Ecclesiastes

All is in vain, says the Preacher...

Chapter 1

Do not try to be clever,
For your cleverness will be undone by fools.
Do not try to be great,
For your greatness will be forgotten.
Do not try to be original,
For everything has been done before.
There is nothing new under the sun.
You may as well try to trap the wind!

Chapter 2

I amassed possessions.
I built houses and undertook landscaping projects.
I became richer than anyone in Jerusalem.
I denied myself nothing.
But I saw that I had gained nothing.
So I tried to acquire Wisdom,
Because the wise man walks in light
And the fool walks in darkness.
But the same fate overtakes both,
So what does it profit me to be wise?

Chapter 3

To everything there is a season
And a time for every purpose under heaven...

Although it may be rather silly
to try to gild this famous lily,
I couldn't leave it without trying...
A time to be born, and a time for dying;
A time to uproot, and a time to sow;
A time to kill, and a time to forgo;
A time to break down, and a time to raise high;
A time to laugh, and a time to cry;
A time to dance, and a time to grieve;
A time to cast wide, and a time to retrieve;
A time to embrace, and a time to refuse;
A time to find, and a time to lose;
A time to save, and a time to spend;
A time to tear, and a time to mend;
A time to speak out, and a time to wait;
A time to love, and a time to hate;
A time of peace, and a time of war.
I don't think there are any more...

PART 2

THE NEW TESTAMENT

PROLOGUE

THE COMING OF THE WORD (John 1:1–14)

The Word, all-knowing and all-seeing,
is John's ingenious invention.
Is it the Principle of Being,
of which God is our apprehension?

The will and working of the Word
engendered all the things we see.
Because of it, the world occurred;
without it, not a thing would be.

It gave mankind the Light we needed
to find the pathway through the night:
before its beam the Dark receded,
but hasn't given up the fight*.

* Or 'hasn't understood it quite'.

God sent a witness, namely John,*
who came before the Light, to say:
'I'm not the one to bank upon –
but he will soon be on his way!'

* John the Baptist.

The lamp, in fact, was being lit,
although the world was unaware
that he who'd helped to fashion it
had, by this time, alighted there.

He came to those of his own kind;
by his own kind he was rejected;
but those who did believe, would find
that they belonged to the Elected.

The Word was given human birth
and dwelled among us for a time:
we saw the Father's Son on earth,
endowed with grace and truth sublime.

CHAPTER 1

THE BIRTH AND YOUTH OF JESUS

The birth of John the Baptist foretold (Luke 1:5–20)

Elizabeth was childless –
a fact that caused her great distress.
Her husband Zechariah and she
had served God long and faithfully,
so this seemed hard, to say the least.
During his turn as Temple Priest,
when Zechariah stood alone
before the altar, he was thrown
to see the Angel Gabriel waiting...
'At last you can start celebrating!'
the Angel said. 'God's heard your prayer.
You'll have a son, who will prepare
Israel's highway to salvation –
a new Elijah for the nation!
John is the name that he will use,
and all strong drink he must refuse.'
'It's everything we could desire,'
exclaimed astonished Zechariah,
'but my wife's past her menopause.'
'Is God subject to Nature's laws?'
came the retort. 'Henceforth be dumb
until the happy day has come!'

(I'll add a postscript to this section
about the family connection
Elizabeth was said to share
with Mary. Thus, the holy pair
of John and Jesus, it would seem,
were cousins in the noble Scheme.)

THE BIRTH OF JESUS (Matthew and Luke)

The stories Luke and Matthew tell
don't fit each other very well.
Few people are aware of this –
most versions are a synthesis...

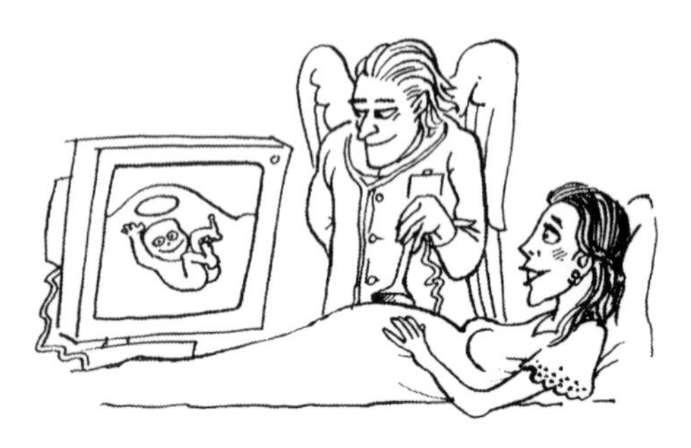

The Annunciation (Luke 1:26–38)

Read *Luke* for the Annunciation –
the Angel Gabriel's salutation
to Mary... 'Hail, most Favoured One,
born to bear Joshua,* the Son
of God on High! You will receive
the Holy Spirit, and conceive,
although you're in a virgin state –
so all you have to do is wait.
He will be great; and when he's grown,
he'll sit upon King David's throne*
for ever.' 'Well, if that's the plan,'
said Mary, 'I'll do what I can!'

* 'Jesus' is the Greek form of Joshua. It would not have been used by Jesus's contemporaries.

* Both Matthew and Luke are at pains to show Joseph's descent from King David through the male line.

Appeasing Joseph (Matthew 1:18–21)

In *Matthew*, it is not explained
if Mary knew what was ordained;
she certainly does not admit
that God has had a hand in it.

When Joseph learns he's been upstaged,
an Angel says: 'Don't be enraged.
Make her your wife! The Son she'll bear
has been the Holy Ghost's affair,
so you can't possibly reject her –
you'll be her husband and protector!
Jesus (her Son) will take away
his people's sin.' 'What can I say?'
thought Joseph, true in word and heart.
But till his birth, they slept apart...

Jesus is born (Matthew's version, 1:24–2:23)

Since Bethlehem was Joseph's native town,
that's where he went with his expectant bride.
She had a home-birth, and they settled down
as man and wife. Meanwhile, some Wise Men tried...

...to find the Child. By following his Star,
they reached Jerusalem, King Herod's seat.
'A Saviour's just been born – he can't be far.
Know where he is? He's someone we must meet!'

King Herod was appalled, but nonetheless
he cunningly pretended to be thrilled...
'When you have found him, give me his address –
I'll worship him!' (Which meant he'd have him killed.)

They found the Holy Child at Joseph's dwelling,
bestowed their gifts, and heard an Angel say:
'Avoid the king, and vanish without telling!'
And so they did. Hearing they'd slipped away...

...the king killed every boy-child under two,
hoping that one of them would be the Threat.*

* The Massacre of the Innocents.

But Joseph had been told what they must do –
decamp to Egypt, and escape the net!

There, for an unknown period, they waited...
At last, in what we now call 4 BC,*
King Herod died, and then they relocated
to Nazareth, up north in Galilee...

* Matthew's version of events therefore means that Jesus was born earlier than 4 BC.

Jesus is born (Luke's version, 2:1–20)

Though Nazareth was Joseph's native town,
he was of David's line, as we have seen.
A census meant they had to travel down
to Bethlehem, where David's roots had been...

While they were there, Mary went into labour.
The pair, so far from home, were in a spot.
No family or friends, no helpful neighbour –
they hadn't even brought a carry-cot!

And so, the humblest place that could be found
became the focus of God's intervention...
A straw-lined manger,* cattle standing round,
and very little media attention...

* Matthew mentions the manger, but not the stable. However, one seems to go with the other.

...until some nearby shepherds had a fright.
An Angel of the Lord appeared, and said:

'A Saviour has been born to you tonight.
They've laid him in a manger for a bed...
...so that will be the sign. Go off and see!'
The skies were heaving with a heavenly throng,
all making most delightful harmony.
Glory to God in Heaven, went their song...

...and peace on earth, goodwill to everyone!
The shepherd, acting on the Angel's clue,
located Jesus, Mary's firstborn Son,
and worshipped him. (That's Version No. 2.)

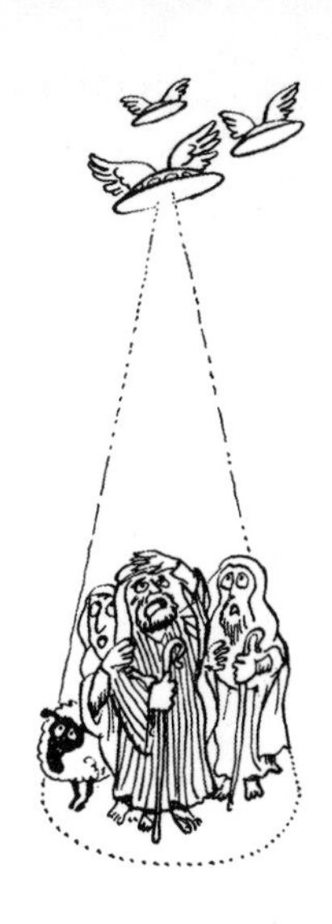

LEFT BEHIND... (Luke 2:41–52)

The Passover Feast
(when their bonds were released
after Pharaoh refused to play ball)*
was a major event.
With a lamb and a tent,
thousands passed through Jerusalem's wall...

* Ex 12.

Joseph, Mary & Co.
would religiously go
every year, with the pilgrims who'd cram
into every last space
in that sanctified place,
and go home again (minus the lamb).

But one year, going back,
they completely lost track
of young Josh (as he would have been known).
Mary, out of her mind,
cried: 'We've left him behind!
Our poor twelve-year-old boy's all alone!'

After endlessly seeking,
they found the lad speaking
near the Temple, in one of the courts.
Their amazement was great
at his skill in debate,
but his mother gave vent to her thoughts...

'That *was* naughty of you!
What a time we've been through!
Three whole days we have sought high and low!'
But Jesus was not
disconcerted one jot...
'You ought to have guessed that I'd go...

...to my Father's address!'
They weren't able to guess
what this meant, although maybe they should.
So they all hit the road
to his parents' abode;
and from that moment on, he was Good.

CHAPTER 2

SOME HIGHLIGHTS FROM HIS MINISTRY

PREPARING THE WAY (Matthew 3, Mark 1, Luke 3)

Meet John the Baptist in full flow!
Down to the Jordan's banks they go
to see this man in camel hair
entreating everyone: 'Prepare!
The Kingdom's almost here! Repent!'
He turns on the Establishment –
the Scripture-quoting Pharisees,*
whom he compares to rotten trees
producing only cankered fruit.
'The axe,' he cries, 'is at your root!
You keep the Letter of the Law –
but it is outward show, no more!
You'll perish in the Judgment Fire!'
'Perhaps this fellow's the Messiah?'
the people ask; but he says 'No!
I'll baptize you with H_2O,
but someone's coming after me
who will baptize you properly,
with Spiritual Fire instead.
He'll stand so high above my head,
I wouldn't dare unlace his shoes!'
That's why he's tempted to refuse*
when Jesus comes to be immersed.
John says: 'Our roles should be reversed.

* The Pharisees get short shrift in Matthew and Luke, but this may reflect the evangelists' bias rather than Jesus's feelings.

* This hesitation is described in Matt 3:13–15.

I ought to be baptized by you,
for you're the greater of us two!'
Jesus won't have it. 'Be advised –
it's by you I must be baptized.'
The Holy Spirit, like a Dove,
descends on Jesus from above,
and God says: 'My beloved Son!'
His Ministry has now begun...

HIS TEMPTATION (Matthew 4, Luke 4)

The Spirit took him off to a Retreat –
a stony place with no means of subsistence.
For forty days and nights he did not eat.
The object was to lower his resistance...

The Devil saw his weakened state, and said:
'I understand you're God's Son? If that's right,
why not command those stones to turn to bread?
You must have worked up quite an appetite!'

Jesus replied: 'Bread's useless on its own.
God's Word supplies a person's inner need.'
The Devil gave up making bread from stone,
and raised his captive very high indeed...

...upon the Temple's dizziest spot. 'Now jump
and see what happens! If you *are* God's Son,
you'll glide to earth without the slightest bump –
or so it's written in Psalm 91!'*

* Verses 11–12.

But Jesus said: 'That cuts no ice with me,
for Scripture reads *Don't put God to the test* –
see Chapter 6 of Deuteronomy!'*
So for the second time he came off best.

* Verse 16.

Now to the third and last act of the drama,
upon a lofty mountain... 'I'll confer
the kingdoms in this splendid panorama
upon yourself, if you will call me Sir!'

But Jesus told the Devil: 'Go to Hell!
It's written that we worship God, not you!
That's found in Deuteronomy as well.*
Out of my way – you're ruining the view!'

6:13.

CALLING HIS DISCIPLES (Matthew 4, Mark 1, Luke 5, John 1)

In *Matthew* and *Mark* we are told
how Andrew and Peter* enrolled
for the team he would use
to spread the Good News.
The brothers were picked when he strolled...

* His birth name was Simon, but Jesus later 'christened' him Peter, so it is simpler to use this name from the start.

...by the Lake.* He called out: 'I need you!
Abandon your nets – join my crew!
You'll be fishers of men!'
Then he walked on again
and chose James and his brother John too...

* The Lake (or Sea) of Galilee.

In *Luke* he amazes them first
by filling their nets till they burst.
Once the catch is aboard,
Peter kneels: 'Oh Lord,
I'm a sinful man – one of the worst!'

Says Jesus: 'No, don't be afraid.
Come with me, and you'll learn a new trade –
there are men to be trawled!'
So, having been called,
they know that he must be obeyed...

But in *John*, as so often, we find
an account of a different kind...
John the Baptist says: 'See!
There's the Lamb, who will be
the Saviour of sinful mankind!'

So two of his students give chase,
and Jesus says: 'Come to my place!'
They go off straight away;
by the end of the day
they're convinced he's endowed with God's grace...

Now Andrew, who's one of the pair,
finds Peter, and tells him: 'Prepare
for a shock, brother dear –
the Messiah is here!
Come and see him – he lives over there!'

But recall that another one went
to see Jesus with Andrew, and spent
a whole day with him too...
We are never told who...
Why doesn't John say whom he meant?*

* Elsewhere, John's gospel refers to 'the disciple whom Jesus loved' without ever naming him. He is believed to be John, one of the sons of Zebedee. Could this be the same person?

The Twelve Disciples

Matthew, Mark and Luke (but not John) list the original twelve disciples, who are later called the Apostles to distinguish them from other 'disciples' or followers of Jesus. The following eleven are included in all three lists. This is Matthew's order:

Peter (Jesus's name for Simon)
Andrew (his brother)
James
John (his brother; both sons of Zebedee)
Philip
Bartholomew
Thomas
Matthew
James (son of Alphaeus)
Simon the Zealot
Judas Iscariot

In Matthew and Mark, the twelfth disciple is Thaddaeus. In Luke, the twelfth disciple is Judas (son of James).

John's gospel mentions Jesus recruiting a disciple named Nathanael, who is not referred to in the other gospels.

After the death of Judas Iscariot, the disciples balloted for the spare place and chose Matthias (Acts 1:15).

THE SERMON ON THE MOUNT (Matthew 5–7)

The Sermon on the Mount is Jesus's most sustained public oration. It includes the Beatitudes (a creed for redemption) and the Precepts (guidelines for a righteous and generally satisfactory life). Within the Precepts is found the core of the modern Lord's Prayer.

There is a much shorter version, called *The Sermon on the Plain,* in Luke, Chapter 6.

1. The Beatitudes

Matt 5:3–12.

The Poor in Spirit will be blessed,
for they will find eternal rest;
the Mourners, who have been bereaved,
will have their sufferings relieved;
and to the Meek (last in the queue)
the riches of the earth are due.

The Saints, who put their faith on trial,
will justify their self-denial;
those who are Merciful, will know
the tolerance they always show;
the ones whose hearts are Pure, will see
the unalloyed Divinity;
the Peacemakers, who challenge Hate,
will be called heirs to God's estate;
and those who suffer Persecution
will earn eternal restitution.
You should rejoice when you are cursed,
for through me you'll be reimbursed –
just like the prophets of the past,
you will find peace in Heaven at last!

2. A few of the Precepts, including the Lord's Prayer

Let Light be seen 5:14.

A light that's hidden from the eye
squanders our energy supply.

Keep cool 5:21.

Though Murder sends you straight to Hell,
a burst of temper can as well.
Embrace those whom you would berate
if you don't wish to share this fate.

Lawyers 5:25.

Avoid the courts, no matter what –
they'll pocket every cent you've got.

Adultery by proxy 5:27.

It's sinful if you don't avert
your eyeballs from a Bit of Skirt.
Though neither stalker nor molester,
it counts as if you *had* possessed her.

Keep your word 5:33.

Why swear an oath? You ought to know
that Yes means Yes, and No means No.

Charitable giving 6:1.

To give should be its own reward.
It will be noticed by the Lord –
but let your fellows witness it
and you'll be judged a hypocrite.

How to pray (The Lord's Prayer) 6:5.

Like giving, praying ought to be
a personal activity.
Short snappy prayers will get through fine
despite the others on the line –
He knows your needs before you do!
I recommend this prayer to you...

Our Father, in your Heavenly state,
receive our praises! We await
the coming of your Kingdom here.
When this will be, we've no idea,
but in the meantime, Lord, we pray,
keep us sustained from day to day;
and even though we're in your debt,
don't ask for settlement just yet –
we'll do the same for those we know,
who can't repay us what they owe!
And stiffen our resistance, when
the Devil troubles us. [Amen.]

Food and clothes 6:25.

Relax, and let it all hang out!
What are you worrying about?
God feeds the birds from day to day –

aren't you more valuable than they?
The flowers of the field are dressed
in what looks like their Sunday best,
their raiment always clean and mended –
why shouldn't you look just as splendid
by letting Him supply *your* needs?
You are more wonderful than weeds!

Your wishes will be answered 7:7.
Ask, and your Father hears you speaking.
Seek, and He knows what you are seeking.
Knock, and the door will open wide
and He will usher you inside.
Though you are far below His state,
you still try to accommodate
your children's wants, and so will He –
however awkward they may be!

THE SECRET VISIT (John 3)

By darkness and a candle flame
a man called Nicodemus came
and spoke to Jesus thus:
'Nobody could dispute your claim
that you are teaching in God's Name –
your signs prove that to us!'

(To have a leading Pharisee
exhibit such humility
is not something that fits

with *Matthew, Mark* and *Luke*. These three
say Jesus was their enemy –
he called them *hypocrites*!)

Jesus responded: 'That is true.
And now you must be born anew –
you'll see God's Kingdom then.'
His guest replied: 'What can I do
to be re-born? I can't pass through
my mother's womb again!

'If mothers must bear children twice
(without some uterine device)
our chance is small indeed!'
'No *earthly* rebirth will suffice
to clear the way to Paradise,'
said Jesus. 'What you'll need...

'...is rebirth in a higher sense,
with *spiritual* ingredients.
If you believe in me,
these quintessential elements
I will accordingly dispense.
Your faith will set you free...

'...to leave behind this mortal ground
and wander where the Spirit's found –
which may be anywhere!
Whence comes the wind? Where is it bound?
We feel it; we hear the sound;
but is it *there* – or *there*?

'I came into the world [he said]
to pierce the Darkness when you're dead,
and overcome the Night!'

But Nicodemus scratched his head,
so Jesus told him: 'Go to bed –
one day you'll see the Light!'

THE BEHEADING OF JOHN THE BAPTIST (Matthew 14, Mark 6)

A party turn that never fails
is taking off all seven veils.*
King Herod's stepdaughter had danced
before his birthday guests; entranced,
the king cried: 'Anything you choose
is yours, my dear – I shan't refuse!'
He very soon regretted it,
but first I must go back a bit...

* Salome's 'dance of the seven veils' has become legendary, but neither the kind of dance nor her name is mentioned in the Gospels.

King Herod's wife, Herodias
(the mother of this comely lass)
had been his brother's wife before.
This contravened Mosaic Law
(Leviticus, Chapter 18).
'She is not legally your queen!'
said John the Baptist – and was jailed.
Now, when the damsel had unveiled...

Verse 16.

...and the inebriated king
had sworn he'd give her anything,
she asked her mother what to do.
'Well, daughter dear, if I were you,
I'd ask for John the Baptist's head
upon a plate!' the lady said.
The girl obeyed, received her wish,
and gave Mamma the tasty dish...

King Herod had been most distressed
about his stepdaughter's request,
because, despite John's fierce invective,
he found his counselling effective,
and used to visit him in clink.*
The news of Jesus made him think:
'John's risen and come back to us –
that's why he's so miraculous!'

* Mark 6:20.

THAT POT OF PERFUME (Matthew 26, Mark 14, Luke 7, John 12)

Two versions of this tale we find
(*Luke's* one is different).
They all report that Jesus dined,
and was deluged with scent...

...a woman poured on him. 'Hang on!'
his team cried, 'that's enough!
[Or so say *Matthew, Mark* and *John*.]
She's wasted priceless stuff!

'Think what the money could have bought
to tackle poverty!'
'But *I'm* unique!' comes the retort.
'The poor will always be!

'My earthly body needs embalming
to stop it going rotten.
Her act was beautiful and charming –
she will not be forgotten.'*

In *Luke* he gets asked out to eat;
a sinful woman's there.

* John's gospel identifies her as Mary the sister of Lazarus, whom Jesus raised from death. She is not named in the others.

She pours her perfume on his feet
and wipes them with her hair...

His host thinks (as he eats his dinner):
'If he's endowed with grace,
he ought to know she is a sinner –
and tell her to her face!'

But Jesus turns on him instead:
'Where was your kiss of greeting?
Or oil to anoint my head?
Your manners take some beating!

'This woman's shown her love for me,
although her sins were great;
and so, thanks to her charity,
I'm going to wipe her slate!

'Your sins are less than hers, I know;
but when your worth is weighed,
you're measured by your love; and so
she beats you, I'm afraid!'

CHAPTER 3

A ROUND-UP OF THE PARABLES

Jesus's reported preaching contains a great many parables (homely stories with a deeper meaning). Faced with the choice of describing the well-known ones in detail, or attempting 'bite-size' summaries, I have gone for the summaries, since the well-known ones are, by definition, already familiar.

I have grouped the parables according to the Gospels in which they appear. Luke is the richest source; the Gospel of John does not contain a single one.

The Parables found in Matthew, Mark and Luke

The Lamp
Why hide a lamp beneath a bed?
Let it shine through the house instead!

Matt 5:14; Mark 4:21; Luke 8:16.

The Mustard Seed
A mustard seed, though very small,
becomes the largest plant of all –
birds perch in its refreshing shade,
because of all the growth it's made.

M 13:31; Mk 4:30; L 13:18.

M 21:33; Mk 12:1; L 20:9.

The Wicked Tenants
A farmer's tenants kept their landlord's portion;
his servants came back beaten black and blue

(or even dead). 'This is bare-faced extortion –
I'll send my son!' But he was slaughtered too...
The owner killed the tenants then and there,
and chose replacements with much greater care.

The Sower

M 13:1; Mk 4:3; L 8:4.

A sower went to sow his seed...
He threw it with abandon!
On stones, on paths, in clumps of weed –
whatever it might land on!
But some reached earth, their roots took hold,
and multiplied a hundredfold.

The Parables found in Matthew and Luke only

The Builder

M 7:24; L 6:46.

A builder does not build a house on sand
unless he is extremely underhand.
A house that's built on rock (like faith in me)
can stand unshaken through adversity.

The Yeast

M 13:33; L 13:20.

The yeast a woman adds to flour
gives it immense self-raising power.
A batch of freshly kneaded dough
is like God's Kingdom – watch it grow!

The Lost Sheep

M 18:12; L 15:4.

Suppose a shepherd hunted for a stray
and brought it safely back... Might he not say:
'I get more joy from this lost sheep of mine
than any of the other ninety-nine!'

*The Wedding Feast**

M 22:1; L 14:16.

* The version in Luke is sometimes called the Great Supper.

The guests were notified, but no one came...
The master told his serving men: 'Invite
the disadvantaged, whether poor or lame,
crippled or blind (or having little sight).
And tell those so-called friends, who slighted me,
they'll do without my hospitality!'

The Wise and Foolish Servants

M 24:45; L 12:42.

A master came back from a spell away...
His man had run things well. 'I'll up your pay!'
Suppose instead the steward had abused
his temporary powers, debauched and boozed,
and generally made the most of it?
If he was caught, he'd end up in the Pit!

The Entrepreneurs (Talents)

M 25:14; L 19:11.

A rich man told each servant to invest
a sum of money, while he was abroad...
On his return, the servants who did best
were given an appropriate reward.
But one did nothing with his master's loan,
and told him why he'd done so, to his face:
'You like to reap what other men have sown!'
'You should have banked the money, in that case,
and earned me interest,' his master said.
'My best investor gets your stake instead!'

The Parables found in Matthew only

The Weeds

13:24

A farmer's crop was full of weeds
a rival sowed among his seeds.
'Don't pull up these invasive shoots –
they'll drag the rest up by the roots!
Leave them until it's time to reap,
then throw the weeds into a heap.'

The Hidden Treasure

13:44.

A man, by careful searching, found
some treasure buried in the ground.
He didn't seize it straight away,
but bought the field in which it lay
by selling off his whole estate.
That is the Kingdom's going rate!

The Pearl

13:45.

A merchant's head was in a whirl...
He'd found an unexampled pearl,
and when he learned what it was worth
he bought it – though it cost the earth!

The Net

13:47.

The Kingdom's net is wide and deep,
its mesh of human size.
The better fish the Angels keep –
the rest, the Devil fries!

The Wicked Debtor

18:23.

A king allowed man *A* (who was his debtor),
to put off paying until things got better.
Then *B*, a man who was in debt to *A*,
explained that he was too hard-up to pay...
A jailed *B*, and this appalled the king,
who tortured *A* till he'd paid everything.

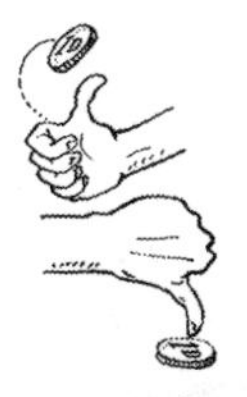

The Workers in the Vineyard

20:1.

This parable has probably caused commentators more headaches than any other, apart perhaps from The Shrewd Steward (p. 170).

A vineyard owner's rate of pay
was one denarius a day.
Since quite a lot of help was needed,
more signed on as the day proceeded;
but all got one denarius...
'They haven't worked as long as us!'

complained the early ones. 'That's true –
but this is what I promised you!'

The Two Sons
A farmer told his sons: 'Help me – 21:28.
I need you both today!'
Son *A* said 'No' but changed his mind.
Son *B* said 'Yes' but then declined.
Those who reject the Word are *B* –
repentant sinners, *A*!

The Wise and Foolish Virgins 25:1.
Five virgins had been wisely trained;
the other five were scatterbrained.
The wise ones kept their lamps alight
while waiting for a feast one night,
thanks to the oil that they had brought.
Their foolish sisters were caught short,
and so their lamps went out... What next?
I've no more space, so read the text!

The Parable found in Mark only

The Seed Growing Secretly 4:26.
A seed grows day and night, without a stop.
Nor does man have to teach it how to crop.

The Parables found in Luke only

The Good Samaritan  10:29.
Love God, and love your neighbour too.
Here's what a neighbour ought to do...
A man was mugged, and left to die.
Two priests ignored him, passing by,
but luckily the desperate man
was seen by a Samaritan
(a race the Jews had come to hate)

who stopped to help him. 'Bear up, mate!
I'll sort you out – get on my steed!'
A neighbour not in name, but deed...

The Friend in Need 11:5.

A man wakes up his friend – he needs some bread...
'Clear off!' his friend calls out, 'we've gone to bed!'
Or does he? No – he'll rise, and do his best
to meet the inconvenient request.

The Man who Lived for the Present 12:16.

A rich man owned a fertile plot
that grew a massive crop of grain...
'I'll build new barns and store the lot,
and never have to work again!'
'Tonight,' said God, 'your lease is due.
What use is all this wealth to you?'

The Conscientious Servants 12:35.

A conscientious staff will always wait
to let their master in, however late.
He'll be so pleased they haven't gone to bed,
he'll say: 'Sit down – I'll serve you all instead!'

The Fruitless Fig Tree 13:6.

A fig tree never bore a crop.
The farmer said: 'Give it the chop!'
His man replied: 'It might be wiser
to try it with some fertilizer!'

The Social Climber 14:7.

If you receive an invitation,
then sit *below* your proper station.
If you should choose a higher seat,
embarrassment will be complete

when your host says: 'Move down a bit –
that is where So-and-so should sit!'
Better be told: 'Your seat's too low!
Come – take the place of So-and-so!'

The Lost Coin 15:8.

A woman loses from her hoard
a coin that she can ill-afford...
She lights her lamp and wields her broom,
and pokes around in every room
until it turns up safe and sound –
then she invites the neighbours round!

The Prodigal Son 15:11.

A younger son took his allotted share
and splurged the lot on women, wine and song...
He ended up a swineherd – in despair,
he trudged back home. His brother thought it wrong
to hold the feast their happy father planned.
'I've slaved for you and got no thanks!' he said.
His father answered: 'Yes, I understand.
But I had grieved for him, and thought him dead.
You must forgive me if I cry for joy
at being reunited with my boy!'

The Shrewd Steward 16:1.

A rich man's steward, who was in disgrace,
sought favour, to obtain another place...
He told two men, who had large debts to pay:
'Reduce the totals – that will be OK!'
The master, when he heard about it, said:
'You've shown initiative, and planned ahead!'

The Rich Man and the Beggar 16:19.

The rich man at his table, and the beggar outside waiting;
but Abraham called the beggar when he died...
The rich man, in Hell's fire, shouted out: 'I'm dehydrating –
bring me a drink!' But Abraham replied:
'A gulf is fixed between us, and it cannot now be crossed.
This man's got all he lacked, and all the wealth you had is lost.'

Master and Servant 17:7.

No servant's told to come indoors
when he has done his outside chores
and eat his dinner! He must wait
till he has filled his master's plate...

The Persistent Widow 18:1.

A Judge who feared not God, nor cared for men,
was pestered by a widow... 'Hear my case!'
Each time he said 'No' she came back again,
till he was sick and tired of her face.
To get a bit of peace, he said 'All right!' –
and made quite sure the plaintiff won her fight...

The Pharisee and the Tax Collector  18:9.

Within the Temple precincts two men prayed...
A Pharisee told God: 'I have obeyed
your detailed regulations to the letter;
I really think no man has served you better!'
A tax collector stood some way apart,
looked down, and murmured with a contrite heart:
'Have mercy on me, Lord, for I have erred.'
His was the prayer that the Almighty heard!

CHAPTER 4

A ROUND-UP OF THE MIRACLES

The Gospels contain more than thirty reports of miracles worked by Jesus, and here is a headlong gallop through twenty-three of the best-known ones. Most occur in more than one gospel, and there are often important differences between the accounts; in fact, it is not always clear if the same miracle is being described.

I have grouped them as follows: *Healing and curing*, *Paraphysical phenomena*, and *Raising the dead*.

Healing and curing

The Centurion's Servant

Matt 8:5, Luke 7:1.

A Roman said: 'My servant's very ill,
but you can cure him by strength of will.
No visit's needed – just say "Let it be!"'
Jesus replied: 'Your faith amazes me!'

The Leper

M 8:1, Mark 1:40, L 5:12.

He healed a leper... 'Don't say what I've done.'
The happy man, of course, told everyone...

The Blind Man

Mk 8:22.

When Jesus spat upon a blind man's eyes,
he made out, to his obvious surprise,
trees walking round. When Jesus spat some more,
he realized it was *people* that he saw!

The Blind of Jericho

M 20:29, Mk 10:46, L 18:35.

The blind of Jericho cried: 'Help us see!'
He did so, as he walked to Calvary...

The Paralytic

Mk 2:1, L 5:17.

So many people crowded round for healing,
friends lowered a paralytic through the ceiling.
Jesus, impressed, loosened his joints once more;
the man departed, this time through the door.

The Gadarene Swine

M 8:28, Mk 5:1, L 8:26.

A man possessed by demons was so strong,
he broke his chains. Then Jesus came along...
'Infect that herd of pigs, and set him free!'
The pigs went mad, and rushed into the sea.

The Issue of Blood

M 9:18, Mk 5:21, L 8:40.

A woman who had bled without remission
just touched his cloak, and cured her condition.

Talk of the Devil

M 9:27.

Some demons had a man's tongue firmly tied,
till Jesus acted... 'Satan's on his side,'
his critics said, when news had got about:
'It's Beelzebub* that turned those demons out!'

* Satan's second-in-command.

The Official's Son

John 4:43.

In Cana, an official told him: 'Come –
my son is dying in Capernaum.'
'No need for me to travel all that way –
he'll start to feel much better from today!'

The Pool at Bethesda

J 5:1.

Each time Bethesda's pool was stirred,
its healing powers were conferred
upon whoever was the first
to reach its edge and be immersed...
A man told Jesus: 'I've been waiting
thirty-eight years – it's most frustrating.

I'm much too slow – what can I do?'
'You could ask *me* to cure you!'

The Possessed Boy M 17:14, Mk 9:14, L 9:37.
Though his disciples did their level best,
they couldn't cure a boy who was possessed.
'A minimum of faith is all you need –
about the volume of a mustard seed!'

Two Blind Men M 9:27.
He healed two blind men... 'Please don't say a word!'
Soon, everyone for miles around had heard.

The Withered Hand M 12:9, Mk 3:1, L 6:6.
One Sabbath, when by strict law work is banned,
he healed a person with a withered hand.
The Pharisees complained, but Jesus said:
'You wouldn't leave a sheep till it was dead
because it fell into a pit today;
a man is worth a lot more, I should say!'

Paraphysical phenomena

The Wedding at Cana J 2:1.
When Jesus turned the water into wine,
I'd like to think the steward said: 'Divine!'

The Fig Tree
A fruitless fig tree teased his appetite...
He shrivelled all its leaves, which served it right. M 21:18, Mk 11:12.

Feeding the Five Thousand...
Five thousand dined off five loaves plus two fish –
each person had as much as they could wish.

M14:13, Mk 6:30, L 9:10, J 6:1.

...and the Four Thousand
Four thousand needed *seven* loaves instead...
Perhaps they gave him less nutritious bread?

M 15:29, Mk 8:1.

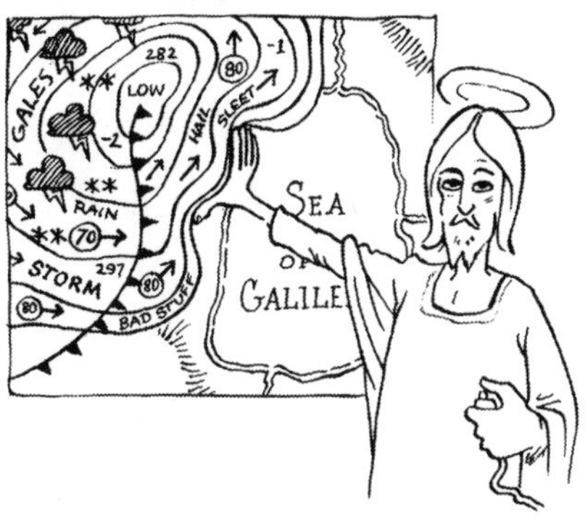

Calming the Storm
A storm blew up when they were in a boat,
and his disciples cried: 'Keep us afloat!'
He woke, rebuked the wind and calmed the deep,
deplored their faith, and no doubt fell asleep.

M 8.23, Mk 4:35, L 8:22.

Walking on the Water
Christ walking on the waves made Peter think
'A piece of cake!' – till he began to sink...

M 14:22, Mk 6:45, J 6:16.

The Miraculous Draught of Fishes
Though Peter's men had fished and caught damn all,
the downcast crew achieved a massive haul
when Jesus said: 'Let down your nets again!'
So Peter altered course, and fished for men...

Luke 5:1, J 21:4.

Raising the dead

The Dead Girl M 9:18, Mk 5:21, L 8:40.

A girl had died; he stood her on her feet...
'Your daughter lives – give her a bite to eat!'

The Woman's Son L 7:11.

At Nain, a funeral was passing by...
He told the corpse's mother: 'Do not cry.'
Her son sat up, engaged in conversation,
and misery turned into celebration...

THE RAISING OF LAZARUS

The circumstances of this celebrated miracle are described in great detail in John's gospel (Chapter 11), and I feel that it deserves special treatment.

There was a man called Lazarus,
belovèd of the Lord.
His sister Mary's known to us –
she was the one who poured...

...the scent on Jesus's bare feet
and wiped them with her hair. 12:1.
His sister Martha (more discreet)
would bustle here and there...

...keeping the household on the go.
Well, Jesus got a note
to say that Lazarus felt low.
'Come quick!' the sisters wrote.

But he delayed for two whole days,
and John has told us why...

He wanted someone *dead* to raise,
to prove we need not die!

When Mary met him on the way,
her face was wet with crying.
'If you'd been here the other day
you could have stopped him dying!'

His human side was undermined
by having to accept
the grief he'd caused. It's here we find
the brief verse *Jesus wept*.*

* 11:35.

The tomb their brother occupied
was sealed with a stone.
'He's dead these four days,' Martha cried,
'so leave it well alone...

'...for putrefaction will have started.'
But Jesus said: '*Believe*!
If you are utterly whole-hearted,
God's glory you'll perceive!'

The stone was moved; he looked aloft.
'Father, these people doubt –
help me convince the ones that scoffed...
Now, Lazarus, come out!'

A cloth was bound around his head,
his hands were bandaged tight...
'Take off his grave clothes,' Jesus said,
'and all will see the Light!'

CHAPTER 5

PASSION WEEK

THE TRIUMPHAL ENTRY INTO JERUSALEM (Matthew 21:1, Mark 11:1, Luke 19:28, John 12:12)

His timetable is set in stone...
The countdown's under way...
He'll give his life, and his alone
in order that he might atone
for all the sin the world has known
until the present day!

He starts the week by borrowing
a donkey as his steed.
Upon the road the watchers fling
their cloaks, to act as cushioning;
palm leaves are waved, and voices sing –
a festive sight indeed!

He enters through the city gate.
The priests are most displeased...

His popularity's so great,
they dare not be precipitate;
so they decide they'd better wait
until he can be seized...

CLEARING THE TEMPLE (Matthew 21:12, Mark 11:15, Luke 19:45, John 2:13)

He went into the Temple court,
where sellers sold and buyers bought,
and drove the whole lot out, upending
the tables used for moneylending,
and knocking all the benches flat
on which the pigeon dealers sat,
explaining, as the chaos spread:
'Remember what Isaiah said? — Isa 56:7.
My house will be a house of prayer –
set up your businesses elsewhere!'
So, what with crowds of people bringing
the blind and lame, and children singing
'Hosanna to King David's Son!'
the priests felt something must be done.
They said: "Those kids are psalming you!'
'Indeed they are. Psalm 8, Verse 2:

By children's lips you will be praised.'
He left them feeling slightly dazed,
and Matthew (not the other three)
states that he made for Bethany,
where Lazarus, some scholars say,
hold told him he could come and stay.

GOOD THURSDAY?

The Passover had come, and that is why
(or so John says) Jesus was meant to die
when all the lambs were offered to the knife –
this symbolized the giving of his life.
But there's an unresolved discrepancy
between John's gospel and the other three...
John writes that it was on a Wednesday night
when they sat down to supper; if that's right,
then *Thursday* was the day when Christ was tried,
brought before Pilate, flogged, and crucified!

Luke, Mark and Matthew put it back a day –
the Passover repast itself, they say
(on Thursday night) was when they sat and ate.
I'll leave you to reflect on this debate...

THE LAST SUPPER (Matthew 26:20, Mark 14:16, Luke 22:14, John 13:1)

That Supper in the upper room...
The table's ready laid,
and only Jesus knows by whom
he's due to be betrayed.

They all recline; he breaks the bread.
'This is my flesh,' says he.
'Do this yourselves, when I am dead,
in memory of me.'

And after that he pours the wine.
This is symbolic too...
'Drink of my blood, in which I'll sign
my covenant with you...

'...despite the fact that one's a traitor!'
'Not I!' they all profess.
(Judas slips out a little later,
but no one seems to guess.)

'In fact, each person at this feast
will fail me in my need.'
Peter protests: 'Well, I at least
am yours in word and deed!'

'Before the cock has finished crowing,'
says Jesus, 'we shall see!
Now arm yourselves,* and let's get going.'
Next stop, Gethsemane...

* Only in Luke. The disciples find two swords, which Jesus thinks will be enough.

THE AGONY IN THE GARDEN (Matthew 26:36, Mark 14:32, Luke 22:39)

Night on the Mount of Olives. Not a sound.
His perspiration dripping on the ground,
God's Son is grappling with his last temptation...
We overhear half of the conversation
as fleshly fear of those impaling nails
consumes him, and his stoicism fails...
'Father, you've filled this chalice, which I'll drink
(just say the word!) – but if, perhaps, you think
it could be taken from my lips untasted,
then take it – though I wouldn't wish it wasted
just to indulge your vacillating Son –
in this, as in all else, thy Will be done!'
John, James and Peter in oblivion lie
not far away, beneath the silent sky...
'Keep watch!' he says to Peter, 'stay awake!
Is that too much to ask you for my sake?
The Spirit's willing, but the Flesh falls short!'
(In Luke, an Angel offers him support.)

He prays again, but now he's given up...
'Father, I know that I must drink this cup –
thy Will be done.' His courage has been tested,
and it is time for him to be arrested...

A THOUGHT FOR JUDAS...

The fact that Judas shopped the Lord
for that argentuous reward*
is universally abhorred...
His treachery's unique!

* Thirty pieces of silver (Matt 26:15).

But what if he'd *refused* to say
that if the priests agreed to pay,
he'd give the Teacher's game away
during that festive week?

The Master Plan would have been wrecked!
How could the armoured guard select
their man, if Judas hadn't pecked
our Saviour on the cheek?

The Gospels state that Jesus *knew*
what this wretch was ordained to do...

He had no choice but see it through!
The Heaven that we seek...

...is ours because the onus fell
on Judas, who betrayed so well
and hanged himself, and went to Hell.
His future's pretty bleak!

THE TRIAL (Matthew 26:57, Mark 14:53, Luke 22:66, John 18:12 & 19)

In *Matthew* and *Mark*
the night was still dark
when the trial of Jesus took place.
The Sanhedrin* had met,
so they were all set,
with false witnesses lined up in case!

* Jewish Council.

But they got nowhere fast,
until two claimed at last:
'We heard this guy say: "I could raise
a new Temple right here –
make the old disappear,
and rebuild it in three working days!"'

'That's a blasphemous claim!'
cried the High Priest (whose name
was Caiaphas). 'Are you the Son

of the Lord God on High?'
'Look up in the sky
and you'll see me, when Judgment's begun!'

A confession like that
knocked Caiaphas flat –
he'd expected a further denial.
So he stood up and tore
the vestments he wore
to signal the end of the trial...

In *Luke* and in *John*
there's much less going on...
Luke waits till the morning has broken.
It's a rapid affair
with no witnesses there,
and in *John* it's no more than a token.

But whatever occurred,
the judgment's transferred
to the Governor. Jesus is brought
before Pilate, to see
if he'll die, or go free.
In the meantime, spare Peter a thought...

PETER DISOWNS JESUS (Matthew 26:69, Mark 14:66, Luke 22:54, John 18:15 & 25)

Credit give where credit's due...
Of that apostolic crew
caught out in Gethsemane,
only Peter doesn't flee,*
staying in his Master's track
when the escort takes him back

* But John says that another (unnamed) disciple accompanied Peter to the High Priest's courtyard.

to the house of Caiaphas.
In the yard, a serving-lass
really puts him on the spot:
'*You* were with that fellow's lot!'
Knowing he could go on trial,
Peter makes his first denial:
'*Me*? I don't know what you mean!'
Even though he has been seen,
he decides he ought to wait
(though he moves towards the gate),
only to be charged again:
'I've seen you among his men!'
comes another servant's shout.
'What are you all on about?'
(That's Denial No. 2.)
Then some men say: 'We know you!
You're a member of his clique –
got to be, from how you speak.
You're from Galilee, like him.'
'By the Holy Seraphim
I don't know the man at all!'
Then he hears the cockerel call,
bringing back his Lord's advice:
'You will have denied me thrice
ere the bird salutes the dawn,
despite the love and faith you've sworn.'

JESUS BEFORE PILATE (Matthew 27:11, Mark 15:1, Luke 23:1, John 18:28)

Pilate governed all Judea,
and he is represented here
as being wholly sympathetic
to Jesus. (This may be cosmetic,

for it is possible, at least,
that he, not Caiaphas the priest,
thought Jesus ought to be suppressed
for causing popular unrest.)*
However, be that as it may,
the Governor is made to say
that Jesus ought to be released...
Each year, at this most solemn feast,
the Romans held an amnesty,
one prisoner to be set free
according to the people's choice.
This time, Barabbas got their voice –
a well-known insurrectionist.
'Oh, very well, if you insist!'
said Pilate, 'so what shall I do
with Jesus – should I free him too?'
With one voice everybody cried:
'We want to see him crucified!'*

* The gospel writers may have wanted to blame the Jews and not the Romans for Jesus's death, so as not to antagonize their conquerors more than was necessary.

* Matthew adds the extra touch: 'Let his blood be on us and on our children' (27:25).

THE MOCKING OF JESUS (Matthew 27:27, Mark 15:16)

The Roman soldiers formed a ring
and dressed their captive like a king.
A crown of thorns, a scarlet cloak,
a reed or bamboo as a joke
to represent his royal staff;
all kneeled, for an extra laugh.
'Hail, king of all the Jews!' they said.
They spat, and struck him on the head,
then dressed him as he was before,
to face the rigour of the law.

THE WATCHERS AND THE CRY (Matthew 27:32, Mark 15:21, Luke 23:32, John 19:16)

There is a green hill far away
outside a city wall,
where our dear Lord was crucified,
*who died to save us all...**

* From the hymn by Mrs C. F. Alexander.

With Simon of Cyrene's help
the Cross is carried there
(he vanishes once he has played
his part in the affair).

They offer Jesus wine to drink,
with gall to dull his senses.
He tastes it, but refuses more,
and so the work commences.

They bang the nails through his hands,
and through his feet as well;
and (quoting from that Easter hymn)
his pain we cannot tell.

Above his head there is a sign –
THE KING OF ALL THE JEWS.
'Come down!' the watching mockers cry,
'you could do, if you choose...

...for you're the Son of God on High –
at least, we *think* it's you!'
A robber hangs on either side,
and one cries 'Save us too!'

'No, mate,' the other felon says,
'we're guilty, you and I –

but he is not!' 'In Heaven we'll meet!'
comes Jesus's reply.

The land is dark from twelve till three;
and then he gives a shout.
But I don't think we'll ever know
exactly what came out...

If you consult Psalm 22,
you'll find the line that's taken
by *Mark* and *Matthew*: 'Oh, my God,
by you I am forsaken!'

Psalm 22:1.

Luke's Jesus is much more resigned.
He just has this to say:
'My spirit, Father, I commend
into your hands this day.'

In *John*, he says 'It is complete,'
then bows his head and dies.
But let me mention something else
that comes as a surprise...

For only here, in John's account,
is Mary on the scene.
The others mention female names
like Mary Magdalene...

...but not the Mother of God's Son –
a startling omission!
Or is it? For she occupied
a marginal position.

Jesus and she did not get on,
or so the text implies.*

* Jesus placed low value on family ties compared with the brotherhood of the spirit (e.g. Matt 12:46), and when a woman says that his mother should be blessed, she gets a sharp put-down (Luke 11:27). At one point his family try to have him put away, thinking he is mad (Mark 3:21).

Did John attempt to patch things up?
Her Son, before he dies...

...tells the disciple whom he loved
to keep her in his care.
'Dear woman, he will be your son,
now I'm no longer there!'

THE ENTOMBMENT (Matthew 27:57, Mark 15:42, Luke 23:50, John 19:38)

When Joseph of Arimathea was told
that Jesus was certified dead,
he requested the body before it was cold.
'I've a brand-new tomb waiting,' he said.

He'd followed the Lord, though in life he'd succeeded;
did he guess that this death was a phase
through which Jesus must pass, and the tomb would be needed
for only a couple of days?*

* In fact only one day and two nights, by most people's reckoning.

Embalming must wait, for the Sabbath was binding,
and at sunset its law would begin.
So he wrapped up the body, and set about finding
a stone to stop thieves getting in...

CHAPTER 6

THE RESURRECTION APPEARANCES

The four Gospels present irreconcilable accounts of Jesus's rising from the dead. It would be impossible to compile a collated version, so I have described them separately.

Matthew (Chapter 28)

The first day of the week was dawning...
Through this defining Easter morning
two women* made their doleful way
to stand before the tomb and pray.
An earthquake shook the ground, and Lo!
down came an Angel, white as snow,
who moved the sealing stone aside.
He told the women: 'Look inside –
Jesus has risen, as you see!
He's on his way to Galilee
to meet with his disciples there.
Please tell them!' The astonished pair
set off, confused by joy and fear –
when who but Jesus should appear?
They clasped his feet in thrilled submission
(which meant he was no apparition),
and he said: 'Tell my waiting crew
to set off for our rendezvous
in Galilee. There we shall meet.'
(The Twelve, of course, were incomplete
since Judas hanged himself, disgraced.)*
They met... He told them: 'I've been placed
in charge of things, here and in Heaven.

* Mary Magdalene and Mary the mother of James and Joses.

* Matthew 27:5.

You are my team, my First Eleven!
Go out and start evangelizing,
for all the nations need baptizing –
invoke the Blessed Trinity
of Father, Holy Ghost,* and Me.
I'll be with all of you, until
the Age ends – as one day it will.'

* Or Holy Spirit.

Mark (Chapter 16)

The first day of the week was dawning...
Through this defining Easter morning
two mournful Marys* made their way
(accompanied by Salome)
to oil the body, even though
they knew the tomb was closed. And lo!
upon beholding it, they saw
the stone was blocking it no more.
They went inside... There, on the right,
a young man sat, arrayed in white.
'Don't be alarmed,' the stranger said.
'Jesus has risen from the dead.
Inform his followers from me
that they're to meet in Galilee!'
The women went off at a run,
afraid to speak to anyone.

* Mary Magdalene and Mary the mother of James.

The earliest known versions of Mark's gospel end at this point. The following verses (16:9-20) appear to be a later addition.

The risen Jesus was first seen
by faithful Mary Magdalene
(he'd exorcized her, long before,
of seven devils). No one saw

the slightest reason to suspect
her crazy story was correct –
and even when two others stated
they'd seen the Lord regenerated,
the thing was treated as a joke,
till Jesus joined them all, and spoke!
'Oh ye of little faith – why doubt
what I explained would come about?
Your job is to evangelize,'
he went on. 'Go out and baptize!
Believe in me, and you will earn
eternal life – if not, you'll burn.
You'll cure people that are ill,
show consummate linguistic skill,
untie the tongues of those possessed,
drink deadly poison with a zest,
and handle snakes.' His message ended,
Lord Jesus left them, and Ascended.

Luke (Chapter 24)

1. The Empty Tomb

The first day of the week was dawning...
On this defining Easter morning

the women* reached the tomb – they'd brought
spices and perfumes of the sort
that halt corporeal decay.
But who had rolled the stone away –
and who had taken him from there?
As they stood gazing in despair,
two men in clothes that shone like lightning
stood in their midst, and looked so frightening
that they were stunned, and fell prostrate...
'You seek the Son of Man? Too late!
Don't you recall his warning, when
he said he'd die and rise again?'
They had forgotten, as you've guessed;
nor did their news convince the rest,
though Peter did go there, and saw
the grave-clothes lying on the floor...

* Mary Magdalene, Joanna, Mary the mother of James, and others unnamed.

2. On the Road to Emmaus

Two servants of the Lord departed
for Emmaus; and once they'd started
(it was a seven-mile trip)
a stranger sought their fellowship,
though neither of the pair suspected
that he was Jesus, resurrected!
'You're talking very earnestly,'
he said, 'please share your news with me.'
'Don't tell me that you haven't heard
about the things that have occurred!'
said Cleopas, one of the two.
'Sorry, I haven't got a clue –
update me!' said the teasing Lord,
and out of them the story poured...
On reaching Emmaus, they said:
'It's getting late – we've got a bed
which you are welcome to tonight,

so come with us and have a bite!'
They brought the stranger to their place;
he took the bread and spoke the grace,
and broke it for them – and they saw
the Jesus they had known before!
He vanished, and the two of them
rushed straight back to Jerusalem...

3. A Last Snack

They found a party had begun...
Their case was not the only one,
for Peter had seen Jesus too!
A voice said: 'Peace to all of you – '
and there he was! They shrank away...
'I am no ghost,' they heard him say.
'Look at my hands! Look at my feet!
Have you, by chance, a bite to eat?'
He tucked in to some fish, then said:
'These things confirm what you have read –
that Christ was due to die and rise,
and here's the proof before your eyes!
Your task you cannot yet fulfil...
Stay in Jerusalem, until
the full Evangelizing Force
descends upon you in due course.'*
Then off to Bethany they went,
and there they witnessed his Ascent.

* This happens at Pentecost (Acts 2:1).

John (Chapters 20 & 21)

1. The Gardener

The first day of the week was dawning...
Through this defining Easter morning
went Mary Magdalene, alone.

Someone had rolled away the stone!
This revelation made her run
to Peter and the nameless one
whom Jesus loved; but all they found
were grave-clothes lying on the ground,
and so they left her there distraught.
Two Angels offered some support
by asking Mary why she cried.
'They've made off with him!' she replied;
but just then, Jesus came to her...
Supposing him the Gardener
(an understandable mistake)
she challenged him: 'Sir, did you take
my Lord's corpse from its resting-place?
I'd like to have it, in that case!'
He spoke her name; she gave a cry
of 'Teacher!' (which is *Rabboni*
in Aramaic). 'Don't touch me,'
he said, 'Although I seem to be,
I'm not completely resurrected –
but tell my brothers I'm expected.'

2. Doubting Thomas

She gave them the amazing news...
They locked the doors against the Jews
and waited as that Sunday passed.
When Jesus came to them at last,
they crowded round the risen martyr,
taking good note of his stigmata
(a Roman soldier slashed his side
when he gave up the ghost, and died).*
But Thomas, absent on that day,
disputed what they had to say:
'I won't believe that form was his
until I touch his injuries!'

* John 19:34.

A week passed after this, and then
they met, and locked the doors again,
and Jesus came... 'Thomas,' he said,
'observe the places where I've bled.
You see my hands? Now feel here,
where someone probed me with a spear –
stop doubting, and believe!' 'I do,'
said Thomas. 'I can see it's you!'
'More blest are those who cannot see,
and still have utter faith in me.'

Like the last few verses of Mark, Chapter 21 of John appears to be an afterthought. It describes a third Resurrection appearance, although only seven of Jesus's disciples are present. The need for a different rhyme scheme will become clear in the penultimate verse.

3. The Miraculous Catch*

'I'm going down to the sea again –
the Sea of Galilee!'
said Peter to the other men.
'Come in my boat with me!

'We'll keep on fishing till it's light,
then count the fish we've caught.'
But after working hard all night,
their total catch was 0.

* With a grateful nod to John Masefield: 'Sea Fever'.

They saw a figure on the shore...

'Had any luck?' it cried.
'You're joking!' 'Well, have one try more –
cast on the starboard side.'

The net was heaving straight away...
'It is the risen Lord!'
cried Peter. Without more delay
he vaulted overboard...

The Saviour had been frying fish,
and asked them for a few.
'Of course – as many as you wish.
We caught them thanks to you!'

The total number in their haul
(153)
does not ring modern bells at all –
but special it must be!

The Lord produced some bread as well:
'Come, join me and partake!'
And so we bid them all farewell,
at breakfast by the lake...

CHAPTER 7

AFTERWARDS...

1. PETER

The Pentecostal Polyglots (Acts 2)

Acts 1 through to 8
set out to relate
the Apostles' first steps on their mission.*
They'll spread the Good News
(and not just to the Jews)
with Peter their leading tactician...

* Acts refers to the Twelve as 'apostles', whereas the Gospels use the word 'disciples' in a rather vague sense to include all Jesus's followers.

But Jesus did mention,
before his Ascension,
that they couldn't begin straight away.*
They would all be assessed;
after that, they'd be blessed
by the Spirit, on some future day.

* Luke 24:49, Acts 1:8.

It came without warning
at nine in the morning
at Pentecost.* They were aware
of a fire that spread

* Or Whitsun.

till it burned on each head,
and they started to speak then and there...

...in voices so loud
they attracted a crowd,
who thought the Apostles were plastered.*
But to each foreign ear
their meaning was clear –
every tongue in the world had been mastered!

* Peter jokes: 'What? Drunk at nine a.m.?' (Acts 2:15).

Peter's built-in translator
now spoke. 'The Creator
sent Jesus, who died thanks to you.
Wash your hands of the blame –
be baptized in his Name!'
Three thousand or so joined the queue...

Notice Peter's technique –
he was careful to speak
of the debt that was owed by the Jews,
whether present or not
at that tragical spot
when Pilate had asked for their views!

2. Curing the Cripple (Acts 3)

Peter played on their guilt
right up to the hilt,
when he cured someone crippled from birth
who was forty years old.
'I've no silver or gold,
but what is such currency worth...

'...against Jesus's name?
No longer be lame!'
The man hopped around in full view

while still holding on
to Peter and John
(who was, it appears, No. 2).

The effect was so stunning
that people came running –
was Peter a fully-fledged prophet?
'My friends, it's not *I*
who was sent from On High
to show you such wonders! Come off it!

'This man stands on his toes
thanks to Jesus, who rose!
All right – you were badly misled
in deciding to plead
that Barabbas be freed;
but Christ's life-blood remains on your head…

'…so repent right away!
The Definitive Day
when God metes out His Judgment, is near.
Declare that you love
the Father Above…
We'll baptize you – that's why we're all here!'

3. Saved by Gamaliel (Acts 5:17–42)

The going got tough
for the priests cut up rough,
and tried the blasphemers in court.
They wanted them dead,
but Gamaliel* said:
'Other fellows have drummed up support…

* A leading member of the Sanhedrin. Paul claimed to have received instruction from him (Acts 22:3).

'…[and he quoted some names],
but despite their great claims,

when they died their supporters dispersed.
Now if God's behind these,
do not anger Him, please –
let's see if they fizzle out first!'

4. Peter's Dream (Acts 10)

In Joppa one day
Peter started to pray,
but he thought he'd like something to eat.
While he waited, he dreamed.
Heaven opened, it seemed,
and let down a thing like a sheet...

In its folds was a zoo
(birds, beasts, reptiles too)
and a Voice said: 'It's true! Eat for free!
Choose whatever I've got
from my *table d'hôte* –
here's wishing you *Bon appetit*!'

'Eat something that crawled?'
replied Peter, appalled,
'or detestable creatures with wings?*
They're completely unclean!'
The Voice said: 'Do you mean
God created *inferior* things?'

* Not all flying creatures were considered 'detestable', but we must assume that the sheet (or tablecloth) contained vultures, bats, etc., which were banned from Jewish tables (Lev 11:13).

The Apostle was caught
by this stinging retort,
and he woke up, not clear what it meant.
However, just then
he was met by three men
whom a soldier, Cornelius, sent...

Would he go to the home
of this high-up from Rome,
who feared God, and incurred great expense
helping people in need?
Peter quickly agreed,
for his vision began to make sense...

He told them all there:
'As you're doubtless aware,
the Law says your house should be closed
to a Jew such as I;
but now I know why
such conditions should *not* be imposed!

'No one is Impure –
of that I am sure.
Let the Spirit descend on this place!'
The Romans praised God
in tongues foreign and odd,
which proved they were filled with His grace.

Peter's Dream thus defined
what God had in mind
regarding the role of His Son.
He died for us all
(though we fly, walk, or crawl).
The Christian religion's begun!*

* Acts 11:26 states that the word 'Christian' was first applied to the community at Antioch.

5. Peter's miraculous escape (Acts 11)

Peter's part of the scene
until Chapter 13,
as the Twelve* risk their lives for the Lord...

* By this time, Matthias had taken the place of Judas Iscariot.

Thanks to public disquiet
and the risk of a riot,
Herod sanctified James* with a sword.

* The brother of John, the sons of Zebedee.

The Jews all approved
when his head was removed;
so Herod eyed Peter as well.
To keep him restrained
he was shackled and chained
with a guard on each side, in his cell...

...till he woke up and saw
all his chains on the floor!
An Angel said: 'Hurry! Get dressed!'
The guards stood aside
and the gate opened wide,
so you can imagine the rest...

There's a steadfast tradition
that he held the position
as head of Rome's Christians. Maybe!
But Acts does not say
if he went all that way,*
although Paul did, as we shall soon see...

* If the First Book of Peter is his writing, he sends greetings from 'Babylon', a common term of contempt for Rome (1 Pet 5:13).

2. PAUL

1. The stoning of Stephen (Acts 6–7)

When a project evolves, and begins to expand,
one secret is *sound delegation.*
Well, soon the Apostles had so much on hand
that they planned some reorganization.

'We'll set up a team to run food distribution
and niggling things of that sort.'
The others applauded this clever solution.
The team should be Seven, they thought...

One was Stephen, a man full of Spirit and Grace;
and when the day's admin was done,
he wasn't afraid to debate face to face
with the opposite camp – guess who won!

At last his opponents could stand it no more.
He was brought to the Council and tried.
He cried: 'Since you killed all the prophets before,
no wonder the Righteous One died!'

He was dragged off and stoned, but he fell on his knees,
asking God if He'd pardon them all,
and praying to Jesus: 'Receive my soul, please!'*
Among his accusers was Saul...

* Stephen is considered to be the first Christian martyr.

2. On the Road to Damascus (Acts 9:1–30)

Now Saul was a Jew of the orthodox type,*
who thought the new faith was a fraud.
Their extravagant claims, and the general hype,
were nothing to do with the Lord!

* A Pharisee.

He complained to the High Priest about them, and said:
'To Damascus I'd like to be sent.
This "Jesus Saves" movement is certain to spread –
we must stamp it out there!' So he went...

...in the hope of a catch of commendable size
to convict and consign to their fate.
But while still on the road, a Light dazzled his eyes –
he collapsed in a terrible state.

'Why persecute me?' asked a Voice, which was heard
by the rest of his company too
(who found him unable to utter a word).
'I am Jesus – I've suffered through you!

'Go on to Damascus, and there you will find
I've arranged an executive meeting.'
His friends led him there (he was totally blind),
and he lay for three days without eating.

A disciple of Christ, Ananias, was told
by the Lord in a vision: 'Please call
at a dwelling on Straight Street, and there you'll behold
a man deep in prayer, known as Saul...

'He wants you to touch him, and help him to see.'
Ananias replied: 'He's a pest!
He's been sent by the priests to snatch people like me,
and put us all under arrest!'

'Don't answer me back!' said the Lord. 'Just obey!
He's the one I've selected to send
to the ends of the earth, to show people the Way –
no longer your scourge, but your friend!'

Ananias laid hands on Saul's eyes, and removed
the dark layer that blinded his sight...
'Jesus Saves!' cried the convert, 'as you have just proved!
Now baptize me, and bring me a bite!'

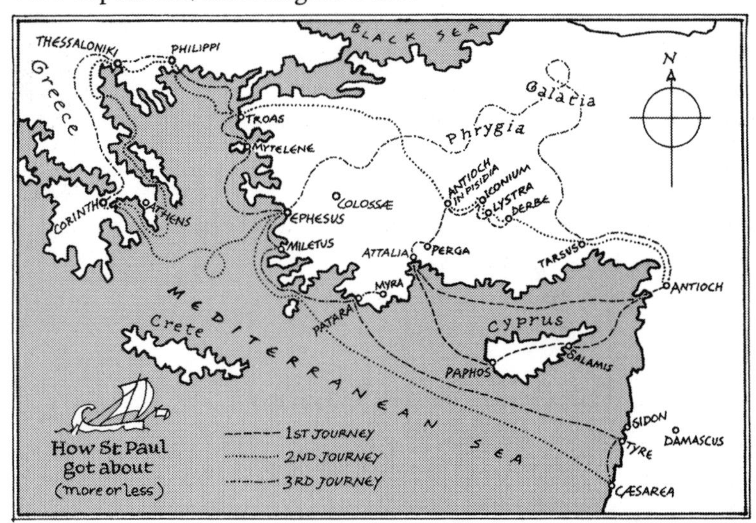

3. Paul's first journey (Acts 13:4–14:28)

Meet Paul (changed from Saul), who's a man with a mission!
The Apostles learned what the Lord planned...
'I'm giving this fellow a roving commission,
with Barnabas lending a hand.'

So they boarded a vessel and sailed away
to the island of Cyprus; and then
they gospelled and preached in what's Turkey today,
till Antioch beckoned again.

4. The Council of Jerusalem (Acts 15:1–31)

Back home, they were plunged into bitter debate
to thrash out a corporate view...
If Gentiles wanted to join the Church – great!
But should they be circumcised too?

In Jerusalem, where the opposing sides met,
the Lord's brother James took the floor.
'That might well put them off – but they ought to be set
some constraints. Jewish butchers, by law...

'...when they slaughter a beast, have to let the blood drain,
which means killing by cutting the throat.
And unnatural sexual acts are profane.
Make them follow these rules!' So they wrote...

...a Letter to Gentiles living abroad,
which stated these terms. (In due course,
though 'unnatural acts' still offended the Lord,
the rules about food lost their force.)

5. Paul's second journey (Acts 15:36–18:22)

On the second long trip, Paul and Timothy* preached
to the Greeks (plus campaigning *en route*).
Thessalonika was the first city they reached,
where the hard-line Jews gave them the boot...

* Paul and Barnabas had fallen out.

...although many believed, and deplored their dismissal.
To Athens and Corinth they went,
and from Corinth, we think, Paul despatched an Epistle –
the first of the Letters he sent.*

* The First Epistle to the Thessalonians.

6. Paul's Epistles...

To cities in Greece: Corinthians, Philippians, Thessalonians.

To cities in Turkey: Colossians, Ephesians, Galatians.

Some Epistles he wrote to the churches he planted
may *precede* all the Gospels in date.
So his view of the Lord very probably slanted
what Matthew, Mark, Luke and John state!

For example, Galatians refers to a split *
that occurred between Peter and Paul,
when Peter (Paul claimed) didn't like to admit
that Jesus had died for us all.

* Gal 2:11.

Paul was sure that no people, whatever their race,
should be cut off from Jesus's Word.
So, without the Epistles to argue his case,
would the Church that we know have occurred?

7. Paul's third journey (Acts 18:23–21:9)

On this very long trip, he sojourned for three years
in Ephesus, teaching each day.
At this juncture, the concept of *relics* appears;
we are told that his handkerchief, say...

19:11.

...would, if touched by the sick, make them well in a trice!
So acquiring saintly possessions
(as a way of receiving their aid or advice)
became one of the Church's obsessions.

On a third floor in Troas, Paul lectured so late
that a young man who perched on a sill
fell asleep, and proceeded to *defenestrate*.*
Paul embraced the dead body, until...

* Fall (or be thrown) from a window.

...it started to breathe, and then went back upstairs
(for he hadn't yet finished his text),
kept on talking till dawn, no doubt offered up prayers,
and set off for the place he'd booked next.

But this tireless man was disturbed by a Voice...
'Jerusalem calls me,' he said.
'Though the Spirit has warned me, I haven't much choice.
I shall end up in prison – or dead.'

The elders of Ephesus wept on the shore
at Miletus (his last port of call).
He said: 'Care for your flock – that's what shepherds are for.
I won't see you again... Bless you all!'

8. Paul's imprisonment (Acts 21–28)

When he reached David's City, false rumours were rife
that he'd ordered Jews living abroad
to be much more laid-back in their everyday life,
downgrading the Laws of the Lord.

He was dragged from the Temple, and would have been killed,
but the Romans retrieved him half dead,
and had got him stretched out to be properly grilled
(i.e., flogged). But at this point he said:

'I'm a *Civis Romanus*, as Roman as you –
maybe more, since your title was bought!*
I've a right to be tried, to decide if it's true
that I'm guilty.' The Romans were caught!

* The Roman commander had paid for his citizenship, whereas Paul was a Roman by birth.

Now, Rome was a city he'd had in his sights*
(though it sounded a dangerous place);
so to get a free passage, he argued his rights
to have *Caesar* be judge of his case!

* He had already written an Epistle to the Romans.

Well, he made it to Rome, and lived under arrest.
Acts comes to an end while our hero
is still going strong; but traditions suggest
that he didn't last long under Nero.*

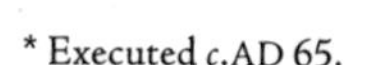

* Executed *c.*AD 65.

9. Some extracts from the Epistles...

*Virtual circumcision (Romans 2:25)**
Those of the Circumcised who God ignore,
debase their fleshly token in His eyes.
But those Unchosen who respect the Law,
He will, by His own favour, circumcise!

* This sums up Paul's belief in redemption by faith alone.

Respect for others (Romans 14:14)
If you are eating out, do not request
a menu item that offends your guest.
Although (in my view) no food is 'unclean',
to put him off his lunch is rather mean.

The Eucharist (1 Corinthians 11:23)
The description by Paul of the Bread and the Wine,
through which Christians can still access Jesus online,
predates all the Gospels (so most people think).
So this Letter of his is our earliest link
with the seismic events of that formative night –
when Saul was arresting all Christians in sight!

On Love (1 Corinthians 13)
Although I utter words that please the ear,
if I speak without love, they're insincere.
And though for prophecy I have a gift,

and though my faith may make a mountain shift,
and I can fathom every mystery,
if I lack love, there is no worth in me.
And though I give my riches to the poor,
and render up my life, you can be sure
that without love, the sacrifice I made
will not reward me for the price I paid.
Love's patient, kind, not envious or vain;
does not proclaim itself, does not seek gain;
endures without complaint, never resents;
delights in truth, dislikes malevolence.
There is no test of strength love cannot bear;
love holds its faith, love never knows despair;
love lasts for ever. Prophets come and go,
tongues falter, knowledge fades; the things we know
we know in part; but when perfection's here,
our comprehension will be crystal clear!
When still a child, I spoke as children do;
I saw things from a child's point of view;
now I have left those childish ways behind,
yet to God's vision I am wholly blind.
A tarnished glass reflects so little light
we hardly see our face; when it is bright
I'll see myself as I myself am seen,
and understand at last what all things mean.
Faith, hope and love abide; but of these three
love is the greatest, and will always be.

Seen by many (1 Corinthians 15:5)
First Peter, then the Twelve, saw Christ upraised;
and then five hundred, who were quite amazed
when they beheld him simultaneously;
then James; then the Apostles; lastly, me.

Not complaining, but... (*2 Corinthians 11:23*)
A lot of people say they've fought for God...
Compared with what I've done, they had it made!
Worked like a dog, thrown into prison, flayed
(five sets of lashes – that's two hundred-odd!);
beaten with rods, stoned, wrecked three times in all;
tossed on the open sea by day and night;
and at Damascus, in Falstaffian plight,
crammed in a basket lowered from the wall...

On his large handwriting (*Galatians 6:11*)
My secretary let me write this bit –
behold the boldness of my Holy Writ!

His stigmata (*Galatians 6:17*)
My body bears the marks that Christ bore too.
So treat me properly – I'm warning you!

Judgment Day (*1 Thessalonians 5:1*)
Re Judgment Day, I haven't got a date.
But be prepared – you haven't long to wait...

Worldly Possessions (*1 Timothy 6:6*)
The world was none the richer for your birth,
nor will it be the poorer when you die.
If you are keen to maximize your worth,
to Heaven's bank account you must apply.

His final message? (*2 Timothy 4:6*)
I have fought the good fight
and my race has been run.
I have tried to do right.
May the Lord say: 'Well done!'

3. REVELATION: The Vision of John*

* With a grateful nod to Samuel Taylor Coleridge: 'Kubla Khan'.

On Patmos, as the Lord decreed,
John revelled in his pleasure trips:
and in these frenzied words you'll read
about the build-up that would lead
to the Apocalypse...

1. The Seven Churches

My first trip [Chapters 1–3]
concerns my dumbstruck confrontation
with *Jesus*! Robed in majesty,
he placed his holy hand on me
and gave me some dictation...

'I've messages for you to write
to seven churches* (see they're sent),
explaining that the End's in sight.
Since this could happen any night,
they really must repent!'

* The churches of Ephesus, Smyrna, Pergamum, Thyatira, Sardis, Philadelphia and Laodicea – all in present-day Turkey.

And so he spelled out, then and there,
how each of them had been assessed...
Performance ratings, wear and tear,
a list of faults they must repair
to keep up with the rest...

2. The Seven Seals, and the Lamb (4–5)

When I had done all that, I saw
the door of Heaven open wide.
The Lord's Voice spoke to me once more
(exactly as he had before)
inviting me inside.

I saw a seated form (guess who!).
Around the Throne, four Seraphim
and four-and-twenty Elders too
came into my astonished view;
and all were praising Him.

The figure on the Throne possessed
a written scroll, which He displayed.
It was with seven seals impressed,
and Saints arrived and tried their best,
but it unopened stayed.

I wept: 'Must it remain unread?'
And then a Lamb with seven eyes,
and seven horns upon his head,
took up the scroll, though he was dead –
which caused me great surprise!

The elders and the beasts prostrated,
and choirs of Angels flew around,
and all the creatures God created
(no matter where they were located)
joined in the heavenly sound...

'O *Agnus Dei,** break the seals!
Your blood saved sinful man!
Please hear our passionate appeals
and find out what the scroll reveals –
if you can't, no one can!'

* Lamb of God.

3. The Four Horsemen (6:1–8)

At last the adulation ceased.
He broke the seals 1–4,
and as he did so, each released
a most apocalyptic beast.
I'll tell you what I saw...

A white horse led this grim quartet –
a new-crowned monarch held the reins.
He had a bow, and seemed all set
on gaining further power yet
through territorial gains.

Then came a horse as red as fire.
Its rider whirled a mighty sword
and had an evident desire
to stir men's passions even higher
till all the nations warred.

A black horse followed. 'Come and buy!'
its rider urged. 'The famine's hit,
and prices have shot up sky-high,
since grain's in very short supply,
and I own all of it!'

A pale horse came fourth and last,
and Death was riding its back,
and as the dreadful mount went past
I watched the spectacle aghast –
for Hell kept in its track...

After recalling the Four Horsemen of the Apocalypse, the writer was disturbed by an unexpected visitor, and the Vision was disrupted. The opening of the remaining seals, the beast whose number is 666, the seven angels, the global cataclysm and the hurling of Satan into a lake of burning sulphur (and much else) were all lost. The last part of the Vision was, however, recovered...*

* A Person from Porlock.

4. The New Jerusalem (21–22)

And lastly, Heaven came in view.
The City, like a bride, descended
and touched the earth, and all was new.
God said: 'I'm going to live here too –
the bad old days are ended!'

And then an Angel let me see
the Holy City close at hand.
Twelve gates in all (in each wall three)
named after Jacob's progeny;
admission, though, was banned...

...to all whose name did not appear
within the Book the Lamb would write.
The sun and moon weren't needed here,
for everything was bright and clear
in God's pervasive Light!

This Book encapsulates my Vision.
If you dare write it out again,
do so with absolute precision –
no editorial revision,
or you'll be damned. *Amen.*

THE END

APPENDICES

Some key passages in the Gospels

The references are to the first verse of the section in the text where the passage is found.

1. THE LIFE AND SAYINGS OF JESUS

	Matt	*Mark*	*Luke*	*John*
The Agony in the Garden	26:36	14:32	22:39	-
The Annunciation	1:20	-	1:26	-
The apostles	10:1	3:13	6:12	-
The arrest	26:47	14:43	22:47	18:1
The baptism of Jesus	3:13	1:9	3:21	1:32
The Beatitudes/Blessings	5:3	-	6:20	-
The beheading of John the Baptist	14:1	6:14	-	-
The birth of Jesus	1:25	-	2:1	-
'Cast the first stone'	-	-	-	8:1
Clearing the Temple	21:12	11:15	19:45	2:13
The Crucifixion	27:32	15:21	23:32	19:16
The Devil tempts Jesus	4:1	1:12	4:1	-
Dining with tax collectors and sinners	9:9	2:13	5:27	-
The empty tomb	28:1	16:1	24:1	20:1
The entombment	27:57	15:42	23:50	19:38

	Matt	*Mark*	*Luke*	*John*
The entry into Jerusalem ('Palm Sunday')	21:1	11:1	19:28	12:12
The flight into Egypt	2:13	-	-	-
Food and clothes	6:25	-	12:22	-
The good shepherd	-	-	-	10:11
The grateful Samaritan	-	-	17:11	-
The greatest Law?	22:34	12:28	10:25	-
Jesus before Pilate	27:11	15:1	23:1	18:28
The Last Supper	26:20	14:16	22:14	13:1
'Love little children'	19:13	10:13	18:15	-
Marriage in Heaven	22:23	12:18	20:27	-
The needle's eye	19:16	10:17	18:18	-
Nicodemus by night	-	-	-	3:1
Peter denies Jesus	26:69	14:66	22:54	18:15
The pot of perfume	26:6	14:3	7:36	12:1
The Precepts	5:13	-	-	-
Preparing the way	3:1	1:1	3:3	1:15
A prophet in his own country	13:53	6:1	-	-
Recruiting the first disciples	4:18	1:16	5:1	1:35
Rendering unto Caesar	22:15	12:13	20:20	-
The Samaritan woman	-	-	-	4:7
Sunday cereal	12:1	2:23	6:1	-
The Transfiguration	17:1	9:2	9:28	-
The trial	26:57	14:53	22:66	18:19
The unforgivable sin	12:30	3:28	12:8	-

2. WHERE TO FIND THE BEST-KNOWN PARABLES

	Matt	*Mark*	*Luke*	*John*
The builder	7:42	-	6:46	-
The conscientious servants	-	-	12:35	-
The wicked debtor	18:21	-	-	-
The entrepreneurs (talents)	25:14	-	19:11	-
The friend in need	-	-	11:5	-
The fruitless fig tree	-	-	13:6	-
The hidden treasure	13:44	-	-	-
The good Samaritan	-	-	10:29	-
The growing seed	-	4:26	-	-
The insistent widow	-	-	18:1	-
The lamp	5:14	4:21	8:16	-
The lost coin	-	-	15:8	-
The lost sheep	18:12	-	15:4	-
The man who lived for the present	-	-	12:16	-
The master and the servant	-	-	17:7	-
The moneylender	-	-	7:36	-
The mustard seed	13:31	4:30	13:18	-
The net	13:47	-	-	-
New wine in old wineskins	9:16	2:21	5:36	-
Patching a garment	9:16	2:21	5:36	-
The pearl	13:45	-	-	-
The prodigal son	-	-	15:11	-
The reluctant guests	-	-	14:15	-
The rich man and the beggar	-	-	16:19	-
The righteous man and the sinner	-	-	18:9	-

	Matt	*Mark*	*Luke*	*John*
The sheep and the goats	25:31	-	-	-
The shrewd steward	-	-	16:1	-
The social climbers	-	-	14:7	-
The sower	13:1	4:3	8:4	-
The tenants	21:33	12:1	20:9	-
The two sons	21:28	-	-	-
The vineyard	20:1	-	-	-
The wedding feast	22:1	-	14:16	-
The weeds	13:24	-	-	-
The widow's mite	-	12:41	21:1	-
The wise and foolish virgins	25:1	-	-	-
The wise and wicked servants	24:45	-	12:42	-
The yeast	13:33	-	-	-

3. WHERE TO FIND THE BEST-KNOWN MIRACLES

Some miracles are referred to in passing. These are omitted from the list.

	Matt	*Mark*	*Luke*	*John*
The bleeding woman, and the dead girl	9:18	5:21	8:40	-
The blind man	-	-	-	9:1
A blind man sees trees	-	8:22	-	-
The blind of Jericho	20:29	10:46	18:35	-
Calming the storm	8:23	4:35	8:22	-
The Centurion's servant	8:5	-	7:1	-
Feeding the five thousand	14:13	6:30	9:10	6:1
Feeding the four thousand	15:29	8:1	-	-
The fig tree	21:18	11:12	-	-
He forgives the paralytic	9:1	2:1	5:17	-
The Gadarene/Gerasene swine	8:28	5:1	8:26	-
The man with leprosy	8:1	1:40	5:12	-
The miraculous catch	-	-	5:1	21:4
The mute	9:27	-	-	-
The official's son	-	-	-	4:43
The paralytic by the pool	-	-	-	5:1
The possessed boy	17:14	9:14	9:37	-
The possessed man	-	1:23	4:33	-
Simon's mother-in-law	8:14	1:29	-	-
The two blind men	9:27	-	-	-
The raising of Lazarus	-	-	-	11:38
Walking on the water	14:22	6:45	-	6:16

	Matt	*Mark*	*Luke*	*John*
Water into wine	-	-	-	2:1
The widow's son	-	-	7:11	-
The withered hand	12:9	3:1	6:6	-
The woman of Canaan/Phoenicia	15:21	7:24	-	-